Alec Clifton-Taylor

Six More English Towns

British Broadcasting Corporation

Published by the
British Broadcasting Corporation
35 Marylebone High Street
London W1M 4AA

ISBN 0 563 20439 7

First published 1981
First paperback edition 1985
Reprinted 1985, 1986
© Alec Clifton-Taylor 1981

Printed in England
by BAS Printers Limited,
Over Wallop, Stockbridge, Hampshire

FOR

DENIS MORIARTY

WHO

IN A SPIRIT OF TOTAL DEDICATION

PRODUCED THE TELEVISION PROGRAMMES

WHICH PROVIDED THE STARTING POINT

BOTH FOR THIS BOOK

AND ITS PREDECESSOR

Acknowledgements

The photographs in this book, apart from those listed below, were taken by Geoff Howard.

Acknowledgement is due to the following for permission to reproduce illustrations (the figures refer to plate numbers): Aerofilms, 24, 56; Beverley Art Gallery and Museum, 230; City of Birmingham Museums and Art Gallery, 7, 9; Ente Provinciale Turismo, Lucca, 57; A. F. Kersting, 53, 54, 217; Leicester City Museum, 26; Leycester Hospital, 15; Dr Alex Moulton, 191, 209, 210; National Monuments Record, 25, 220; Hon. Robin Neville, 128, 129; Saffron Walden Museum, 88, 89; Warwick Town Council, 42.

Contents

Photographs by Geoff Howard

2. Saffron Walden: Old Sun Inn, Church Street

Introduction

Like its predecessor, this book originated in a series of television programmes for the BBC, but what is right for television is not necessarily right for the printed page, nor perhaps should be; the material has in fact been not only considerably expanded but substantially recast.

The choice of towns was, as before, extremely difficult. The first essential was a good geographical spread. But many other factors had also to be taken into account, in the interests, as I described in the earlier introduction, of balance. All the towns chosen had to be comparatively small, but they could be hilly or flat, colourful or monochrome, planned or unplanned, classical or romantic. England can offer an abundance of good candidates.

What needs to be said at once is that the present six are in no sense 'second strings'. Their average quality seems to me to be every bit as good as that of the first six. If I were asked, for example, why Warwick was not included in the first set, the answer would be very simple: because we had Ludlow! On analysis, these two places offer several striking resemblances. Both are dominated by a big castle perched high up above a curving river. Both have a very large and notable parish church with a lofty tower. Both, for different reasons, are partly planned towns. Both combine plenty of stone (mainly sandstone) buildings with an abundance of timber-framing and many excellent Georgian houses in brick. It seems to me difficult to say positively which is the finer, but it is evident that they could not both have a place in the same series.

But, especially in the field of traditional building materials, which have long been a special concern of mine, it has been possible in this second series to branch out into new fields which the earlier set did not touch. Pargeting, for example (2), or 'mathematical' tiles. And, to take another aspect, how many English towns display massive Elizabethan fortifications? The answer will emerge: one, and one only.

In their overall shape, these towns differ considerably. Lewes and Beverley are long and narrow (in both places I shall explain why); Berwick and Saffron Walden are tightly-knit and compact. But what these towns all possess is homogeneity. Where local building materials remain supreme, differences of architectural style matter hardly at all. Often, indeed, they add interest to a street. What is, however, absolutely vital in such towns is that the overall character of the place should be respected. It is not necessary, nor even desirable, as a rule, that new buildings should imitate their older neighbours, but they must harmonise with them, and respect their scale. That is why the Civic Amenities Act of 1967, which launched the Conservation Areas, was and is so very important. 'Where architectural beauty still reigns,' wrote Walter Godfrey, when he was Director of the National Buildings Record (as it was then called), 'it is as much an economic as an aesthetic loss to take any part of it away.'

The greatest enemy of all these beautiful old towns is undoubtedly traffic: not local traffic, which is seldom a serious menace, but through traffic, 'ruthless in its demands and so indifferent to the damage it inflicts', as Godfrey added. He was writing over thirty years ago; today the situation is infinitely worse. How is this problem to be tackled?

The one course which should *never* even be contemplated is street widening. I will stick my neck out, and say to those responsible for looking after our old towns that, if there is one immutable rule to be observed everywhere, this is it. Through traffic *must* be diverted from old towns and excluded altogether from certain streets or areas. No other way is possible. There should be more one-way streets and more streets for walkers only, closed to traffic entirely. Shopkeepers in such streets seldom suffer and often benefit, but it is of course a great advantage if there can be vehicle access from the back. If not, it must be allowed up to, say, 10 am.

In at least one of the towns discussed in this book, Lewes, the traffic situation is no longer nearly as bad as it was, thanks to a really bold move, the construction of a quarter-mile-long tunnel to the east, in addition to the southern by-pass. At two others, Beverley and Berwick, by-passes which will give both places a wide berth are now under construction. But at Warwick the through traffic is now an appalling menace, and vigorous action to counter it is still awaited.

The principal aim of this book is the same as that of the programmes on television: to give pleasure by assisting visual awareness. If some readers find themselves becoming more critical as a result, there will be no harm in that. For there is still so much left to be enjoyed. Despite all the mistakes and misfortunes of the last hundred and fifty years, England's heritage of worth-while buildings is still prodigious. Sir Nikolaus Pevsner and his collaborators needed forty-six packed volumes just to describe it.

And happily, more and more people care. For me it was a special pleasure, when we were making the television programmes, to meet some of them, and in every one of these towns we received the most generous and disinterested local help. Civic Societies flourish now as never before, and they have a most important role to play, both constructively and also as watchdogs. Amenity societies, too, recruit more and more members every year. As a result, and although there is certainly no room for complacency, it is undoubtedly much more difficult than it used to be for greedy and unscrupulous developers and others to 'get away with it'. Government grants towards the restoration and rehabilitation of buildings worth saving are now also available; and among these six towns Berwick, as we shall see, has been a notably enterprising beneficiary.

For in the last resort it is always the townspeople themselves who must make the efforts. I would therefore beg every reader who has cause to be proud of his (or her) own town to play as active and vocal a part as possible in its preservation.

3. Bradford-on-Avon: Bradford Lock,
Kennet and Avon Canal

4. Warwick Castle

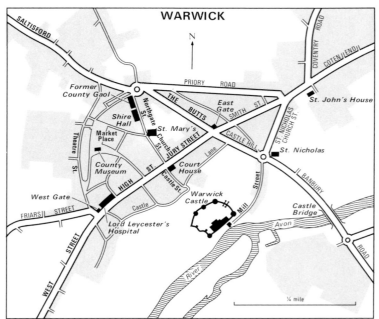

1. Warwick

Where exactly the centre of England may be is difficult to determine, for there is no agreed formula for measuring it. The towns which are closest to the centre are Coventry, Kenilworth, Leamington and Warwick, all in Warwickshire. What is not open to argument is that this is England's most centrally placed county: the hub of the wheel, as it were. Warwickshire's waters feed the Severn, the Trent, and even to a very small extent the Thames too; no other county is as distant from the sea.

So I start this book in the heart of the Midlands, and it was indeed a Queen of Mercia, Ethelfleda, daughter of Alfred the Great, who founded the town of Warwick in the second decade of the tenth century. The place prospered: 244 houses are recorded in the Domesday Survey, a few of which were later removed to provide space for a market place. When Leland visited the town in 1539, he found it 'right strongly ditched and walled, having the compass of a good mile within the wall'. The East and West gates, both crowned by chapels, were well preserved, as in fact they still are.

But far and away the largest and most imposing building is the Castle (4) perched on a precipice that drops a sheer fifty feet into the River Avon. It is one of the great sights of England, and the king-pin of the Warwick story: 'very strong both by nature and by art,' as William Camden put it, rather neatly, in his *Britannia* of 1586. Its dramatic site, its huge scale, its tremendous towers: all these are features which have fascinated many generations of artists, and not least Canaletto, whose two splendid paintings, done about 1749, were part of the Castle's collection for over two hundred years but are now, very appropriately if they had to leave their original habitat, in the City Art Gallery at Birmingham. The picture of the East front from the Outer Ward (7) has Caesar's tower on the left and Guy's tower on the right, and between them the Clock tower, preceded by a barbican, built for additional defence. The other one (9) shows the same front from inside the courtyard. Compared with the impeccable state in which they are maintained today (6), (10), both views look quite informal. They had no mowing machines in Canaletto's day.

The Castle is the first building in Warwick of which there is any record. This goes back to 915, when Ethelfleda erected a fort here as a protection against the incursions of the Danes; but even the exact site of this is uncertain. The Castle was refounded in 1068 by William the Conqueror and, during the three succeeding centuries, greatly enlarged. In the course of history no fewer than six families have held the Earldom of Warwick. It was to the Beauchamps, Earls of the second creation, that the greater part of what is to be seen today was originally due. They held the Earldom from 1267 until 1449. It was Thomas Beauchamp, Earl from 1331 to 1369, who built Caesar's tower, 147 feet high, on a solid rock directly above the river; and he was also the builder of the Clock tower, which was the gatehouse, and the wall linking them. Guy's tower,

6. Warwick Castle, East front

7. Canaletto, Warwick Castle, East front

6

7

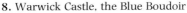

8. Warwick Castle, the Blue Boudoir

128 feet, was the work of his son, also Thomas.

Ann Beauchamp, the family's heiress, married Richard Neville, Earl of Salisbury, known to history as the Kingmaker. Thereby, in 1449, he also obtained the Earldom of Warwick. He was the Chief Minister of Edward IV, but was slain at Barnet in 1471. His daughter married the Duke of Clarence, who now acquired the Castle, and was created Earl of Warwick by his brother. Clarence added the North gate and began the Clarence tower to the west of it, but before this was finished he was charged with high treason and probably drowned in a butt of Malmsey wine. The Castle then went to his brother, afterwards Richard III, who began the Bear tower to the east of the North gate: this was never completed.

In 1547 the Castle was granted to John Dudley, who was made Earl of Warwick, but this line died out in 1590. The Grevilles, present holders of the title, did not appear on the scene until 1604. Fulke Greville was created Lord Brooke by James I. By this time the Castle's condition was ruinous; the towers were used as the county gaol. But the Grevilles were determined to make it, in the words of the eminent seventeenth-century antiquary Sir William Dugdale, 'the most princely seat within the midland parts of the realm': and they did. It was they who made it habitable again; only the basement and undercrofts partly preserve their medieval character. Otherwise, the domestic range is entirely Jacobean or later, and mostly later: the Cedar Drawing Room, dating from about 1680, is splendid. It has an elaborate coffered ceiling, painted cream and gilded, five beautiful chandeliers of Waterford glass, and gilt Rococo sconces. The Little Blue Boudoir (8) has an equally sumptuous ceiling characteristic of this date and an explosion of succulent fruit over the fireplace. The Great Hall and several adjoining apartments had to be reconstructed after a serious fire in 1871, which accounts for the unmistakably Victorian appearance of part of this building today, especially externally on the courtyard side.

The Grevilles did not become Earls of Warwick until 1759. A few years before that — in 1749, to be precise — Lord Brooke (as he then was) had the percipience, or the good luck, to employ the

9

10

9. Canaletto, Warwick Castle, the Inner Ward

10. Warwick Castle, Inner Ward, looking east

11. Great Bridge

landscape gardener Lancelot ('Capability') Brown. It was probably the very first commission of his independent practice. He planted several thousand trees, including a thousand oaks, and swept away the old, stiff, formal gardens. He also masked the town, so completely that within this large estate one is totally unaware of its existence. A couple of years later Horace Walpole was there. 'I saw Warwick,' he wrote to George Montagu on 22 July 1751; 'a pretty old town in the form of a cross, small and thinly inhabited. The castle is enchanting; the view pleased me more than I can express. It has been well laid out by one Brown. One sees what the prevalence of taste does. Little Brooke, who would have chuckled to have been born in an age of clipped hedges, has submitted to let his garden and park be natural.'

It has to be said that there is a reverse side to this coin. It is almost certainly true that this park would not have been nearly as lovely as it is if it had been left to the townspeople. But the fact remains that the Castle and its park monopolise the whole of Warwick's view of the Avon. Except when they cross Castle Bridge, the citizens of Warwick could live their lives in total unawareness of the lovely view at their gates.

The eastward extension of the demesne was secured by an ingenious bargain between the Earl and the townspeople. From medieval days all the traffic coming into Warwick from the southeast had to cross the Avon by a long narrow bridge comprising fourteen arches. By 1789 this bridge was in such a bad state of repair as to be adjudged unsafe. The Earl saw his chance. If, he said, the people would agree to divert some 250 yards upstream the road from Banbury, which climbed the hill right under the Castle's east wall, he would defray three-quarters of the cost of a new bridge. It required an Act of Parliament to get the scheme through, but the bargain was struck. Thereby the Earl acquired an invaluable extension of his grounds; but the town certainly obtained a beautiful new bridge (11) with a single span of 105 feet. The designer, a local man, William Eborall, was inspired by that fine bridge designer, Robert Mylne, who a few years before had erected within the park Leafield Bridge, which was badly damaged some years ago by a falling tree. The Great Bridge, as it is known,

12. View from Castle roof, with the Great Bridge in the distance

was completed in 1793, which was only just in time, for shortly afterwards several arches of the medieval bridge were swept away by a flood. The rest survives as a picturesque landscape feature, of which a plunging view can be obtained from the Castle roof (12).

The Castle no longer belongs to the Grevilles, but it is still privately owned. In 1978 it was acquired by Madame Tussaud's, who have changed very little, and keep it warm in winter and open to the public all through the year. Even the peacocks, about thirty of them, flaunting their magnificent plumage, still strut around, shrieking with delight and now and again paying social visits to neighbouring houses.

William Camden wrote of this town: 'It stands upon a hill, which is one entire rock of freestone, out of whose bowels were wrought all the public buildings that adorn it.' The Castle was built of this local sandstone and so were the town walls, the gates and the various churches; but until the seventeenth century very little else. The medieval town must have been constructed almost entirely of wood, plaster and thatch. But in 1694 disaster struck.

The month of September, after a dry summer, was always a propitious time for fires. The Great Fire of London, of 1666, burned from the third to the sixth. Nine years later, on 20 September, another fire devastated the town of Northampton. Warwick's turn came nineteen years after that. What happened is described in a letter dated 9 September 1694 from the people of Warwick to their Diocesan, the Bishop of Worcester:

> About two of the clock in the afternoone, on the fifth of September, a fire broke forth in the western part of the Town, which by a violent and tempestuous wind then blowing from the south west, was soe swiftly carried through the principal and chief tradeing parts of the Town, that within the space of half an hour, severall places, and farr distant from each other, were all in flames at once, soe that all endeavours that could be used to hinder the fierceness of its progress were vain and ineffectual, and within the space of four or five hours it had wholly consumed (except two or three houses) all the High Street, Sheep Street and Church Street, part of Jury Street, New Street and many buildings about the Market Place, together with (the most lamented loss) the great and ancient church of Saint Maryes, and severall lanes and buildings in other parts of the Town; and with them a very great part of the goods of the Inhabitants, not only of those whose houses were totally ruined, but many others whose houses were adjoining thereunto.

In a slightly later letter, appealing for money, it is stated that the fire 'consumed the houses of above 250 families, many of whom were the principal and chiefest traders of the town, together with their shops'.* In the Museum are exhibited a large model which attempts to show what the town looked like before the Fire, and a plan showing the extent of the devastation. From this it is evident that, with a few exceptions, it was really only the buildings on or near the periphery that escaped. So that is where the timber-framing is; and quite a lot of it has managed to survive.

The most pleasing example is the early Elizabethan house of Thomas Oken (13) in Castle Street, which is now a museum of old

*For these quotations, and for other kind help, I am indebted to Mr Michael Farr, FSA, the County Archivist; they occur in his unpublished paper, *The Fire of Warwick, 1694.*

13. Oken's House

14. 39–47 Mill Street, looking west

15. Leycester Hospital, Courtyard, *c.* 1860

16. Leycester Hospital, the Master's House

dolls and toys. Oken, a well-to-do mercer who died in 1573 and who, with his wife, is commemorated by a pretty little brass in the church, was a very likeable man. He left all his considerable property to Trustees appointed to act for the poor of the Borough. Structurally this house exhibits timber-framing at its most satisfying, with two splendidly robust curved braces echoed by two smaller ones, no longer black.

Mill Street, which completely escaped the Fire, has many timber-framed houses, the fronts of which are not in fact all as old as their owners would probably like us to believe they are. But at the far end, on the left, is a range which composes into a picturesque group (14).

There is plenty of timber-framing to be seen just inside the West Gate. The Fire started close to this point in some cottages at the back of the Friends' Meeting House, but the wind was blowing the other way. So one of Warwick's most famous buildings, Lord Leycester's (as it is usually spelt here) Hospital (18) also escaped. This was founded in 1571 as an almshouse for 'such poor and impotent persons as shall be maimed or hurt in the wars in the service of the Queen [Elizabeth I] or her heirs and successors, but some of the buildings are older than that, for they were originally the premises of two guilds, established as early as 1383. So within are two halls, one of which, in 1546, became the Council Chamber for the Corporation. The Earl of Leicester persuaded the Council to make a move, in order that he could establish his Hospital; and an

17. Leycester Hospital, Malt House

18. Leycester Hospital and the West Gate

19. Tudor House Inn, West Street

almshouse it has been ever since. There is a complete courtyard, and adjoining it to the right, the former Anchor Inn has been incorporated, together with another building behind this, known as the Malt House (17). This has a double jetty (or overhang) and some of that rather 'busy' infilling, with cusped circles and concave-sided diamonds, which often characterises timber-framing in the Midland and Western counties.

By the 1840s the Hospital had been allowed to fall into a very dilapidated state, and a great deal of reconstruction took place. The front of the Master's house on the far side of the courtyard (16), one of the parts most often photographed by unsuspecting visitors, is an addition of about 1850 and a complete sham. What purports to be timbering is for the most part only plaster, painted black and made to look a little more convincing by being given a slight projection from the plane of the wall surface. The pattern was derived from the Malt House. This façade steps out several feet in front of the original elevation in order that passage communication could be provided, upstairs and down, between the rooms. Some of the original windows, blocked, can still be seen inside the house, in the inner walls of these passages.

The timbers of the Leycester Hospital have had a decidedly chequered career. Oak, provided that it has a damp-proof base and an overhanging roof – a good hat and a good pair of shoes, as they used to say in Devon – will last for centuries, and often becomes still harder in the course of time: stronger even than some varieties of stone. It requires no protective covering; on the contrary, in fact, oak needs to 'breathe'. Nevertheless, when the Master's house received its new front, all the timbering in the courtyard was given a coat of red ochre, as can be seen in a watercolour of the time preserved in the Hospital (15). Later, the red gave way to black and the pale yellow ochre infilling to white, at a time when, especially in the West Midlands, this more strident colour scheme became all the rage.

In recent years, a good deal has been learned about the best ways of treating timber-framing. De-blacking is now the order of the day, and the whole of the exterior of the Leycester Hospital has been given this treatment, to its great artistic benefit. Even though, it has to be said, there is too much cement in what should be a lime plaster infilling, the pale ochre colouring is a great improvement on the white. On the other hand, the retention of the assertive black and white scheme on the front of the Master's house can be justified, since the 'timbers', being largely plaster, would always have had to be painted; and although they could now become red-brown again, for a Victorian building 'black and white' is historically correct. And, it must be added, the taste for it dies hard in England's 'Middle West'. Many people there still dote on it.

Warwick can still show a handful of typical examples. One, Victorian in the centre but with Elizabethan gables to either side, directly faces the Leycester Hospital (20). The adjoining building, in the eighteenth century, when exposed timbers were decidedly unfashionable, was given a coat of roughcast. This became so dilapidated that it was decided to remove it. The timber frame that was revealed comprises only verticals and horizontals. Such formal reticence, unusual in this part of the country, is to some eyes very welcome: and it is certainly all the better for not being black. It is a pity that in both these houses more care has not yet been taken over the windows. Although of two disparate patterns, how much more pleasing are the windows of the Tudor House Inn (19) in West Street. This, contradicting its name, is Jacobean or a little later. Despite large-scale restoration, this building, erected on a sandstone plinth, has not lost its picture-book appeal. A less emphatic colour scheme might be preferred (it is today very black and white), but the quartet of gables and the very straightforward roof covered with plain hand-made tiles are delightful.

20. 41–45 High Street

21. Friends' Meeting House, High Street

There is no shortage of stone here; on the contrary, as Camden observed, the town stands upon it – Triassic sandstone. But unhappily none of it is very good. It is an attractive stone when first quarried, but distressingly friable. It is not capable of enduring centuries of weathering. The present condition of the quoins at the Friends' Meeting House (21), which are not much more than 200 years old, is not untypical.

Stone would hardly seem to have been used here for domestic architecture before the Stuart period, and then only very sparingly. The first important stone house in Warwick was St John's (22) in 1626. It occupies the site of another medieval hospital, using that word in its original sense of a place that dispensed hospitality: 'casual lodging and refreshment to poor wayfarers and more permanent help to the local poor and infirm'. At the Reformation, here as in so many other places, the poor and infirm were sacrificed to upstart ambitions. A royal servant, one Anthony Stoughton, obtained from Henry VIII the grant of this property, and in due course the old buildings, including the chapel, were demolished.

22. St John's House

The house that took their place is certainly a great ornament to the town, and is now a charmingly presented annexe to the County Museum; upstairs is housed the museum of the Royal Warwickshire regiment. Being well to the east of the town centre, it luckily escaped the Fire.

But the fabric is in constant need of attention. The buff-grey sandstone almost certainly came from Coten End, a quarry no more than half a mile away, which, with permission, can still be seen, although it is no longer worked. This attractive-looking stone was always decidedly on the soft side. While it retained what the masons called its quarry sap, it could be cut like cheese. So through the years a great deal of the stonework has had to be renewed; and unfortunately this is a continuing requirement.

The County Museum itself occupied the old Market Hall (23), another of the small number of pre-Fire stone buildings in Warwick. It was begun in 1670, and may be compared with the admittedly more accomplished contemporary example at Abingdon by Christopher Kempster, one of Wren's master-builders. This one was by a Warwickshire man, William Hurlbutt. Until 1879 the ground floor was open, as the designer intended. Then it was filled in, with windows which are visually a disaster. The upstairs windows were originally casements, but are all the better for being Georgian. In 1935, incredible as it may seem, the Town Council actually wanted to demolish this building, as obstructive to the market. Happily, wiser counsels prevailed; and in 1961 the cupola and dormers were put back. This greatly improved the appearance of the building. Nevertheless the condition of the stonework is not all that could be wished.

When the building ceased to be a Market Hall and became a Museum — in the first place, of the Warwick Natural History Society — it was, I suppose, inevitable that the ground floor had to be glazed in, regrettable though this was from the architectural standpoint, the more so as the present scheme of glazing is so outstandingly inept. It became the County Museum in 1951. Every county should have its museum, and most of them do. A local museum has a quite specific function, which is to display things concerned with the locality and little or nothing else. If there are good local artists, like, for example, the Devis family at Preston, so much the better. But we do not visit a local museum in search of, shall we say, a lithograph by Picasso. Internationally known artists could only be represented by prints or maquettes or very minor works anyway. Here everything is concerned with Warwickshire, including cases devoted to local geology, local flora and fauna, and so on. The display is highly effective. The building is certainly on the small side for its purpose, and a new one is contemplated. But I am not sure that this would be, on balance, an advantage. With the addition of St John's this seems to me to be a very comfortable size for a local museum, and its central situation

23. County Museum, Market Place

is excellent. When the need for more space becomes really pressing, the best solution might be for the soldiers to relinquish the upper floor of St John's and for the regimental museum to be housed elsewhere.

Also of stone, as mentioned above, were the town walls and gates. Of the walls, which were much strengthened in the fourteenth century, little now survives beyond a stretch adjoining the West Gate. But the Gate itself is very striking, especially from outside, as the road rises quite steeply to reach it, and above the gate there is not only St James's Chapel but a robust tower added early in the fifteenth century. The chapel is largely a Victorian re-creation by Sir George Gilbert Scott, but not unattractive and in daily use. It is now incorporated in the Leycester Hospital, but from within the walls it can be seen on the left of plate 18.

The East Gate (25), dating from the beginning of the fifteenth

24. The town from the air, looking south-east

25. The East Gate

century, also carries a chapel, dedicated to St Peter, and with its rather amusing and most original tower this is the focal point of Jury Street. But it is not medieval: the old chapel was nearly all rebuilt in 1788 by Francis Hiorne, a local architect and builder, three times mayor of Warwick, who specialised in Georgian Gothic and is perhaps best known for his excellent rebuilding, a few years earlier, of the church at Tetbury in Gloucestershire. The East Gate chapel is now used as an art room by the adjoining girls' school.

Close to both these gates are small but rather precious survivors: two Greek Doric cast-iron pillar boxes with vertical apertures (26). The first letter boxes had been erected in England in 1853, and in the early days local authorities were left free, within reason, to produce their own designs; they were not even always red. Not many, though, went in for the Classical style, and still fewer, like Warwick, have kept a couple of them.

The High Cross, which is presumed to have been, as at Chichester and elsewhere, in the form of an open canopy carried on eight stone piers and surmounted by a cross, was not so fortunate. For although without Roman connections, Warwick, like Chichester, Chester, Gloucester and a few others was planned on the cruciform principle (24), with one straight stretch, High Street and Jury Street, linking the West and East Gates, as it still does (5), and the other climbing from the old Bridge and continuing to the Church and on to the no longer existing North Gate beyond. (The diversion of this road with the opening of the Great Bridge in 1793 has already been described.) The Cross, needless to say, was at the point of intersection, as at Chichester it still is. But after the Fire the act for the Rebuilding of the Town of Warwick, passed in December 1694, declared, among other things, that henceforth 'all public streets and lanes should be of a convenient wideness', and this particularly applied to the High Street-Jury Street vista. For this the High Cross was regarded as an obstruction, so in October 1695 it was removed (41).

26. Victorian letter-box at the West Gate

28. St Mary's, Beauchamp Chapel

Today there is a far worse obstruction: the unceasing traffic, to which this straight stretch between the West Gate and the East Gate acts of course as an irresistible magnet. To this subject I shall return.

Despite the statement in the letter to the Bishop of Worcester, quoted earlier, that the fire had consumed 'the great and ancient church of Saint Maryes', part of that church did in fact escape. The nave and transepts were destroyed and so was the tower, but the eastern parts survived: chancel, chapter house and the burial chapel of the Beauchamps. Architecturally, therefore, the church is a curious hybrid (27).

St Mary was always a very big church, and became collegiate (that is to say, served not just by a single priest but by a whole group or college of them) as early as the twelfth century. In the course of time it assembled a fantastic collection of relics, which included, improbably enough, a fragment of Moses' burning bush and some of the oil in which fire came down from heaven at Pentecost, not to mention a drop of the Virgin Mary's milk. More endearing, perhaps, and surely more useful, was the frying pan of St Brandon. At the dissolution of the college in 1544, the burgesses of Warwick were granted possession, except of the Beauchamp Chapel at the south-east corner.

27. St Mary's Church from the south-east

28

29. St Mary's, on jamb of East window in Beauchamp Chapel, St Margaret

This chapel, which took twenty-one years (1443–64) to build, is what everyone goes to see (28). Henry VII's Chapel at Westminster and St George's Windsor apart, it is perhaps the most lavish family burial chapel in the country: it is providential that it escaped the great conflagration. The architecture, it is true, might be described as sumptuous rather than sensitive; the design of the large windows with their depressed arches looks somewhat mechanical, and the lierne vaulting, for all its panoply of bosses, some very large and all coloured crimson and gold, is, compared with many others, decidedly coarse. The unpleasing reredos is no part of the original fittings (it was designed by Butterfield), and the Flemish stained glass, made by John Prudde, glazier to the King, suffered grievously from Puritan fanaticism in 1641. But some of the sculpture is remarkable. The east window is unusual in having no fewer than thirty little figures in the hollows of its moulded frame: they surround it and run up both the principal mullions. Most of them are angels, but there are also a few larger female saints which, in their present chocolate-box colours, might almost have stepped out of one of those lovely rococo churches in Bavaria. St Mary Magdalene (29) stands upon a dragon.

Of the tombs, much the most impressive is that of Richard Beauchamp, guardian of the child King Henry VI, who built the chapel to house it; his monument is placed plumb in the middle, as his will specified that it should be. The material of the tomb chest is Purbeck marble, of the sculpture gilded brass. The effigy itself was modelled by William Austen of London, not from life but fifteen years after the Earl's death, and is not a portrait; the sculptor was simply commissioned to produce a figure of a nobleman in armour (31). He scored a memorable success: the effigy is both strong and elegant. It is not easy to forget the wonderful hands. Set within the canopied niches below, and also in gilded brass, are fourteen figures of weepers (30) wearing heavy mourning cloaks and modelled with great sensibility, alternating with eighteen little, rather mass-produced angels. Each of the mourners, seven peers and seven ladies, is identified by a shield lower down, executed in coloured enamel.

30. St Mary's, Tomb of Richard Beauchamp, Weepers and angels

The other tombs in the Beauchamp Chapel are by no means as good, but tucked between this chapel and the chancel is the lovely little Dean's Chapel (32), inserted a few years after the Beauchamp Chapel had been completed. This has a fan vault with pendants; the bosses are gilded and the spandrels painted blue. The niches to either side of the window are crowned by damaged but prodigiously intricate canopies. One of them even has a fan vault which echoes in miniature that of the chapel itself. But alas, in 1641, Colonel Purefoy, the local Puritan fanatic, and his henchmen shattered all the figures which once peopled these exquisite creations.

Although the Fire did not spare the stalls, the chancel itself was otherwise saved. It is entered under a very lofty arch; the Victorian stained glass renders it rather dark. The vault, not a rich one, has flying ribs which, although not very attractive, are slightly sensational. The furnishings are mostly Victorian, but in the centre of the chancel is another Beauchamp tomb, this time of Thomas, the Black Prince's guardian, who was in command at Crécy and died in 1369, seventy years earlier than the founder of the Beauchamp chapel. The effigies of Thomas and his wife, in alabaster, are decidedly stiff and unnotable as sculptures; round the sides of the chest are no fewer than twenty-six little mourners, interesting for their fourteenth-century costumes.

The nave (34), completed in 1704, is what the Germans call a *Hallenkirche* or hall church: the type of church, not at all common

31. St Mary's, Effigy of Richard Beauchamp

32. St Mary's, the Dean's Chapel

34. St Mary's, Nave

in England, in which the aisles are the same height as the nave itself. So we experience a great sense of space. The architect for the rebuilding was not Sir Christopher Wren, who submitted a scheme, but Sir William Wilson. He was born the son of a Leicester baker, and was not knighted for his architecural achievements, but through the influence of a rich widow, Lady Pudsey, who fell in love with him in his thirties and married him. Nevertheless, his designs were preferred to Wren's. I do not believe that Wren could conceivably have created window tracery as ugly as this.

The tower, which is frequently but mistakenly attributed to Wren, is best seen at a distance. It is very well placed, but this was a lucky accident. It was started farther east, flush with the west ends of the aisles. But when that tower had risen twenty-nine feet above the nave roof it developed alarming cracks, probably because of the poor quality of the stone, some of which is known to have been quarried in the churchyard itself. So there was nothing for it but to take down what had been built and to begin again on firmer foundations with a better stone, brought from Shrewley, five miles away to the west. Scenically this was fortunate, for from every direction this big tower, 174 feet high and aslant to the axis of all the streets that converge on (33), composes very well indeed. The silhouette is excellent. The road used to pass beneath it. Close to, though, it emerges as a very odd stylistic hybrid, with repetitive 33 niches up every face and a most curious crown.

33. St Mary's, Tower from west

35. Shire Hall, Northgate Street

36. 7–9 Northgate Street, formerly the Judge's Lodgings

None of Warwick's other medieval churches survives. Most of St Nicholas, well sited close to the Great Bridge, was rebuilt in 1779 – 80. It is a very early example of the Gothic revival style, and not good. St Mary is the only church in this town worth visiting. It furnishes the principal link between pre-Fire and post-Fire Warwick.

Northwards from St Mary runs what has been described as the most handsome Georgian street in the Midlands: Northgate Street. The left (west) side was wholly given over to 'the majesty of the Law'. The former Judge's Lodgings (36) come first: a model of simple dignity, dating from 1814 – 16. The whole front is ashlared, but since the grander rooms are upstairs, the ground floor is visually strengthened by the introduction of banded rustication and prominent keystones, to either side of an Ionic porch. The windows have the large lights and very thin elegant glazing bars typical of this date.

Adjoining this house is the Shire Hall (35), and beyond this the former County Gaol. Northgate Street was only partly burnt in the Fire: the old Shire Hall escaped, and was not rebuilt until the 1750s, while the Gaol dates only from 1777–83. Once again the local sandstone wore badly, so much so that these two buildings have had to be completely refaced: the Shire Hall in 1946–8 and the Gaol soon afterwards. This was done in Hollington stone from Staffordshire; the colour is fawn with a faint blush of pink. This was

37. Former County Gaol, Northgate Street

the best, indeed almost the only Triassic sandstone still procurable, and it was undoubtedly the correct choice. For complete refacing it is satisfactory, but on the side wall of the old Gaol can be seen the unfortunate effect of patching Warwick stone with Hollington.

Although both ashlar-faced and superficially similar, these two classical buildings are in fact very different. Appropriately enough, it is the Shire Hall which has much the richer detailing. There are a rusticated base, moulded architraves and pediments for the windows, Corinthian capitals, and carved swags of fruit and flowers on the frieze and on the pediment to either side of a heraldic cartouche. The adjoining building (37) became a Barracks for the Warwickshire Militia in 1861 and now provides offices for the County Council; but its original use, as the Gaol, determined its character. So here the Order is not Corinthian but Doric, and there is no ornamentation at all; this is neo-Classicism at its most austere. Unfortunately all the windows have been replaced by modern metal casements, and their proportions changed. The new plinth here is of Hornton stone.

The interior of the Shire Hall is specially notable for the two octagonal Court Rooms (38), both lit from above, with many of their original furnishings. Both have galleries behind free-standing Corinthian columns, and the eight-sided dome of the Crown Court is adorned with stucco panels of two alternating designs (1). If you have got to do a stretch, you could hardly wish for a more elegant *point de départ*!

38. Shire Hall: Crown Court

39. Former Court House, Jury Street

The next building needing external refurbishing (in 1960) was the former Court House (39), finished in 1728, and now the offices of the Town Council. This was the work of Francis Smith, who gave additional weight and authority to what is really a comparatively small building by rusticating the stonework horizontally throughout, and by making a feature of the keystones over each window. The duplication of the end pilasters was a favourite device of classical designers to provide points of punctuation, as it were. A stern figure of Justice occupies the central niche, with the Royal Arms above and the Arms of Warwickshire below, both admirably carved. Aloft, thanks to a Government grant, is a restoration of Smith's open balustrade, which in the nineteenth century had been replaced by a solid parapet. The building greatly benefits from this: and so it should, for it is one of the town's most delightful

40. 10 Market Place

40

41. View of Town and Castle from St Mary's church tower, with former Court House in the foreground

possessions. The principal room inside is the one upstairs, known as the Ball Room, which is now let out for functions. It is a handsome room, but mistakes were made when, twenty years or so ago, it was redecorated: when the necessary funds become available, an expert should be called in to give it back its lost elegance.

Francis Smith, generally known as Smith of Warwick (42), was Mayor of this town in 1713 and again in 1728. He is a good example of a phenomenon not uncommon in the eighteenth century: a man of humble birth — his father was a bricklayer — who started life as a stonemason and gradually went up in the world. In middle age, like many of us, he put on a good deal of weight. It was the Fire that gave him his chance: he became a master-builder and presently, in all but name, an architect. His substantial practice all over the Midlands included such major country houses as Stoneleigh Abbey, Chicheley Hall and Sutton Scarsdale. He was no genius, but at its best his work, whether in stone or brick, makes a considerable impact.

A house in the Market Place at Warwick, No. 10 (40), although undocumented, was almost certainly his work, not only for stylistic reasons but because it was built, in 1714, for his father-in-law. Here again the local sandstone was used, which decayed so badly that, to save it, complete refacing was undertaken in 1963. The big Corinthian pilasters and the modillioned eaves cornice provide a strong frame within which, as usual with Smith, there are three tiers of windows set into moulded architraves, in this case with projecting 'ears'. The principal windows, with prominent keystones, are all segmental-headed, and so is the pediment over the door. Beneath the windows on the first and second storeys are aprons in the form of raised and moulded panels. The plinth has banded rustication; the hipped roof has good hand-made tiles, three prominent dormers with pediments of alternating design, and symmetrically placed chimneys. Not one of these features is peculiar to this house, but none is other than wholly appropriate and handled with complete assurance. The house is therefore a great ornament to the Market Place, even though its full effect has in recent years been marred by joining it on to a modern building which is totally incompatible with it.

After the Fire, timber-framing and especially thatch were absolutely taboo in Warwick; in some streets, in fact, any thatch which had not been burned was prescribed as 'a common nuisance' and had by law to be removed. So the choice here lay only between the local sandstone, easy to quarry and to shape but of questionable durability, and brick.

A stone house built early in the eighteenth century which has so far managed to survive with no more than a limited amount of repatching is 8 Castle Street (43). It doubtless owes its relatively good condition to the fact that it faces east-north-east; stone buildings with their backs to the prevailing wind have always been less vulnerable to decay. From 1826 this house served as the 'Dispensary for the Sick and Poor of Warwick and its Neighbourhood', and it is still a doctors' surgery and clinic. The only unexpected feature is the design of the capitals, both of the doorway and of the end-pilasters: these are flat but fluted, with

42. Francis Smith

43. 8 Castle Street, the 'Dispensary'

44. Centre part of 10 Church Street

delicate ornamentation. Although all of them are set within plain reveals without architraves or keystones, this house offers an interesting study in windows. The thin, finely moulded glazing bars on the ground floor are an obvious renewal, perhaps about 1820. On the first floor the thick flat bars are original: glazing bars were nearly all like this when they first came in, shortly before 1700. And then in the dormers there are casements with leaded lights, a reminiscence of the seventeenth century, when everybody had windows like these.

By comparison with this modest but very likeable country cousin, 10 Church Street (44), occupied by the Warwick and County Club and not a hundred yards away, is brimming over with self-confidence. This was built about a generation later; but unfortunately it faces into the prevailing wind, so the stonework has suffered in the most dire fashion, and the upper storey was partly renewed early in the nineteenth century with Roman cement. However, there is still much to enjoy. The glazing bars of the windows are just right; and so is the counterpoint between the bold rustication of the lower storey and the smooth upper storey, with its delicate twin pilasters and pair of small engaged columns at the centre. Above these runs a neat band of guilloche ornamentation, while the capitals present a stylisation of the acanthus leaf, far removed from nature. There is a balustraded parapet crowned by four ornamental urns, and behind, a good roof of dark red hand-made tiles. Only the door seems rather unworthy. It is quite dwarfed by the imposing triple window with the glazed tympanum flowing into the pediment above. Seldom perhaps does a classical design manage to be as friendly – almost, it might be said, as beguiling – as this one.

By this time, however, brick was rapidly becoming the favourite building material. It had indeed been used in Warwick a little before the Fire. Landor House (46) adjoining the East Gate was

45. 24 Castle Street

46. Landor House, Smith Street

built in 1692–3 by Roger Hurlbutt, who was either the son or the nephew of the William who was responsible for the Market House; and fortunately the Fire did not reach as far as this. The material is brick, with stone employed only for the dressings. It has a good deal of wood too, notably the boldly projecting modillioned eaves cornice typical of the later Stuart period. The modillions (brackets) here are carved, and the egg and tongue moulding running along the base furnishes additional enrichment. But the prominent doorcase, which might be assumed also to be wood, is in fact of painted stone. The great weakness, from the design standpoint, is the windows. These would originally have been casements, with leaded lights. The existing windows were put in about a century later, probably by the parents of the poet and essayist, Walter Savage Landor, who was born here and after whom the house, which is now part of a large girls' school, is named. Admittedly the window apertures are not of the right proportions for the usual Georgian sash windows. But they should have been reglazed with three, not two, lights across and five, not four, up (three by three in the dormers). If this were done, the visual improvement would be quite remarkable. Perhaps some of the girls would undertake the task as a labour of love? The cost would not be prohibitive: and every lover of fine architecture would be grateful to them.

At 24 Castle Street (45) the windows could have been converted to double-hung sashes more easily, as the openings are not far from 'standard Georgian'; but here all the iron casements with rectangular leaded lights have survived. The house escaped the Fire and may well antedate it by a few years, although listed (wrongly, surely?) as eighteenth century. It is an agreeable building, but unfortunately now divided; no doubt it was when this occurred that the two central windows were blocked up. The dressings are again in the rather soft local sandstone, which, for better preservation, has had here to be painted. It is a pity that the two owners do not agree to have a common colour-scheme. In their own interests this would add scale and dignity to their property. The one on the right, from which the ugly pipes have now been removed, was not long ago repainted a light stone colour in order to approximate to the original colour scheme; but the other one, now 2 Castle Lane, is the more lively of the two. With red brick, white paint often looks best.

Northgate House (48), built in 1698, recalls the town's vanished North Gate. It would seem from the outset to have been designed as two houses: the grandest semi-detached imaginable, with a shared carriage entrance in the centre. It may well have been put up as a speculation. The windows were originally all casements, each with a wooden mullion and a transom, and at the back a few of these can still be seen. There are two old sundials: one with an oval face, in the central pediment, and the other on an elaborately corbelled projection, to the right.

It was now four years after the Fire, and there was a big demand

47. 6, 4 and 2 Northgate Street

for bricks in Warwick. It did not take long to discover that on the surrounding commons there was plenty of earth suitable for brickmaking, so brick-kilns were set up, and there seems to have been quite an influx of itinerant labour.

When they were first built, the Georgian houses on the east, the less grand, side of Northgate Street (47) were regarded as among the most desirable in Warwick. Today the County Council occupies nearly all of them. Red brick was employed throughout, but, regrettably, the majority of them were later stuccoed over; presumably this happened early in the nineteenth century, when,

48. Northgate House

even if one could not have stone, it was fashionable to aspire to it,
and ruled trowel lines on stucco, which all these houses had, could,
it was thought, suggest blocks of masonry. The modern over-
assertive dormers are also to be regretted. Otherwise, these are
good houses: Nos. 6 and 4 still keep their original brick fronts, and
No. 4 its old tiles too. Every window has its glazing bars, and over
the doors are charming fanlights. The pilasters on the left-hand
side of Nos. 2 and 4 are an interesting indication of post-Fire
nervousness, for they mask the ends of exceptionally thick party-
walls. The Act for the Rebuilding of the Town of Warwick decreed
that walls were to be eighteen inches thick at ground-floor level,
thirteen inches at the first floor and eight inches higher up. It
legalised the banishment from the principal streets of 'all noisome
trades, especially those perilous in respect of fire'.

Mill Street, which runs down from the church of St Nicholas to
the remains of the old bridge, was, as I have said, unaffected by the
Fire. So into this predominantly timber-framed street a brick house
could be regarded as an intruder. It is: yet what a welcome
intrusion! No. 15 (Millers Place) (49) could well be regarded as the
most enjoyable of any here. It is of red brick set off by white-painted
dressings. And, as an extra bonus, there is still Crown glass in
almost all the windows. This hand-spun glass, virtually unobtainable for over a century, harbours the most delightful, glinting
reflections.

The material prosperity of the nineteenth century involved the uglification of many towns, not only in England but all over the world. The towns that came off best, visually, were those like Warwick which did not expand very much. But it is hard to think of any other place with a frontispiece to its Gas Works as elegant as that which happily still survives here (50) in the street called Saltisford. It is of brick, faced with Parker's Roman cement, and painted white. The date is 1822. Though no longer the Gas Works, these are still commercial premises, which must give pleasure to every visually aware person who passes this way.

From the Victorian period the town emerged comparatively unscathed; but recently it has not been so fortunate. In the aftermath of the lamentable rearrangements of 1974, Warwick is today in the anomalous situation of being no longer a Borough but just part of a District Council administered from Leamington, and yet still the County Town of Warwickshire. And the new County Council Offices, opened in 1973, are, alas, the eyesore of the town. They had, presumably, to be very large, but was it necessary to site them so conspicuously? The approach from the north-west, with the tower of St Mary dominating the skyline, used to offer one of Warwick's most delightful views. This has been totally destroyed.

In this matter the damage has been committed; and there is nothing more that can be done. The County Council can at least be commended for not having added a tower block, which in Warwick would have been a crime. The great problem of the future is how to control the volume of traffic. Most of it would appear to be through traffic, and it is already a scourge.

With really determined action on the part of the authorities, I am convinced that a viable solution could be reached, and at no very high cost. Comparable results have already been achieved elsewhere: at Cirencester, for example, and at Huntingdon. The historic town, bounded by Castle Lane, Theatre Street, Barrack Street and the Butts, is quite small: only half a mile each way. From

49. 15 Mill Street

50. Former Gas Works, Saltisford

this area heavy freight vehicles, except for local deliveries, and even buses should be totally excluded, and, by a judicious arrangement of one-way streets and a little pedestrianisation, cars should also be strongly dissuaded from passing through this area. It could be done, and without the construction of an inner relief road on the north side of the town, which has aroused a great deal of well-justified opposition and would anyway be a costly undertaking. If these arrangements were introduced, people would not be prevented from driving into the shopping area; on the contrary, with the riddance of the through traffic, it would be much easier and more pleasant to do just that. Car parking in certain streets, including the Market Place, would have for the present to remain. It is the through traffic which is the great menace.

In 1716, twenty-two years after the Fire, Daniel Defoe wrote: 'Warwick is now rebuilt in so noble and beautiful a manner that few towns in England make so fine an appearance.' Of some streets, even today, that is still largely true. Not long ago though, Warwick was disfigured by some of the ugliest street lights in England. After a while, it is good to record that most of the lamps were changed, decidedly for the better. But this incident is sufficient to illustrate what harm can be done by wrong decisions, probably now taken in Leamington by people who may not fully realise what a treasure Warwick is. Constant vigilance is required. Only if enough people care, and are prepared if necessary to make an almighty fuss to ensure that their views are heard and regarded, is the character of this rather vulnerable town likely to be preserved.

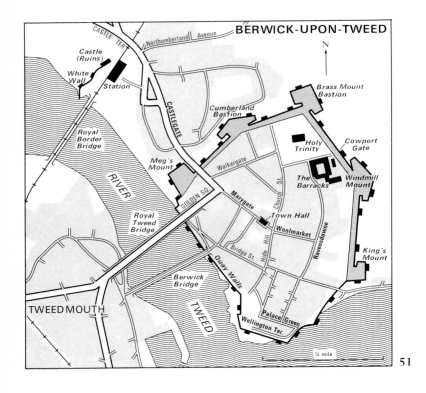

BERWICK-UPON-TWEED

N

Castle (Ruins)
White Wall
Station
CASTLE TER.
Northumberland Avenue
Royal Border Bridge
RIVER
CASTLEGATE
Meg's Mount
Cumberland Bastion
Walkergate
GOLDEN SQ.
Marygate
Royal Tweed Bridge
Church St.
Brass Mount Bastion
Holy Trinity
Cowport Gate
The Barracks
Windmill Mount
Town Hall
Woolmarket
Ravensdowne
Bridge St.
Hide Hill
King's Mount
TWEEDMOUTH
Berwick Bridge
Quay Walls
Wellington Ter.
Palace Green
TWEED
¼ mile

51

52. Old Bridge

2. Berwick-upon-Tweed

To approach Berwick from the south, whether by road, by rail or from the sea, is a memorable experience. The lovely Tweed, flowing down from the heights above the small town of Moffat, has broadened here to estuarial proportions. What a natural barrier. What a natural *frontier*! Yet, coming from this direction, Berwick is on the far side. Should it not be in Scotland?

It was: until 1174, and six times thereafter. The place changed hands no fewer than fourteen times between 1174 and 1482, when it finally became English. In medieval days it was truly Britain's shuttlecock. After 1482 it became a free town, with its liberties (as they were known) stretching for about three miles along the coast northwards and four up the Tweed. But several more centuries were to elapse before this frontier town, the most northerly in England, could be correctly described as being in Northumberland.

Exactly when is a nice question, to which there is no simple answer. In the treaty of 1502, between Henry VII and James IV of Scotland, Berwick had been acknowledged as an independent state, 'of' the kingdom of England but not within it. Until the Wales and Berwick-upon-Tweed Act of 1746, general Acts of Parliament did not apply to Berwick (nor to Wales) unless they were specifically mentioned. Another Act, passed in 1836, constituted Berwick and its liberties together with Tweedmouth and Spittal, across the river, as a county of itself, and this Act was not repealed until 1974, so legally it was only then that the town became part of Northumberland. But for all practical purposes (and how typically English to leave the question of legal status unresolved) Berwick had been included in Northumberland long before this; nor, according to the Foreign Office Library, after a detailed scrutiny of the relevant documents, is there any truth in the oft-repeated assertion that the declaration of the Crimean War was made in the names of England, Scotland and Berwick-upon-Tweed. In 1885 the town became one of Northumberland's Parliamentary constituencies and four years later responsibility for its roads and bridges passed to the new Northumberland County Council. In 1920 it ceased to have its own police and separate education services, and its own Quarter Sessions came at last to an end in 1951.*

Nor do the anomalies end here. Until 1844 the territory opposite Berwick, on the south side of the Tweed, was not part of Northumberland either. Who, I wonder, has heard of Islandshire, or of Norhamshire, of which Norham was the capital? I certainly had not, until I began work on the history of Berwick. These two 'shires' were, it is said — though there is no documentary authority to support it — given by King Oswald in the seventh

*For helping me to resolve this complicated question, and for all the factual information in this paragraph, I am greatly indebted to Mr Robin Gard, Northumberland's County Archivist.

53. Union Chain Bridge, Loan End

century to the See of Lindisfarne, centred on Holy Island, some ten miles to the south-east (just visible to the right of the tower in 64). What is certain is that in due course they formed part of the patrimony of the Cathedral Church of Durham, and after the Reformation became an integral part of County Durham, the Bishop having alienated the See's manors to Queen Elizabeth I. Tweedmouth and Spittal, as mentioned above, were incorporated with Berwick in 1836; eight years later the rest of these peculiar little shires were absorbed into Northumberland.

The origins of the town of Berwick are obscure; but by the twelfth century it was of sufficient importance to be designated by David I (1124−53) as one of the Four Royal Burghs of Scotland. The others were Roxburgh (of which nothing now remains beyond the scanty ruins of the castle), Edinburgh and Stirling. However, in 1174 William I of Scotland, having invaded Northumberland and been captured at Alnwick, had to surrender Berwick to the English as part of his ransom. By then there was a wooden bridge across the Tweed, the first of many, for this river is liable to tremendous floods. It was swept away in 1199. Two replacements were needed during the thirteenth century. The first was again of timber, the second of stone. But it was of no avail. The stone bridge was destroyed in 1294 after a life of only nine years. Thereafter, for over two centuries, there was again no bridge at all. In Tudor times another wooden one was erected, the condition of which was frequently dangerous. James I journeyed this way to London in 1603. He was alarmed by its shaking and expressed the hope that a new stone bridge would soon replace it, for which in due course he was persuaded to find the money.

This bridge, Berwick Bridge or the Old Bridge as it is now known, took twenty-three years to build, but its construction was extremely sound, and it still stands (52). When it was finished in 1634 it became the pride and wonder of the town: 1164 feet long with fifteen arches of very varying spans, which can still carry extremely heavy loads. The channel here is at its deepest close to the Berwick shore, which explains the steep rise to the second arch, under which there had to be sufficient head-room for small sailing boats. After that there is a long gradual descent to the Tweed-mouth bank. The width is only about 18 feet, but each pier has cutwaters crowned by recesses for walkers. The sixth pier is larger than the others: this was the boundary point between Berwick and Islandshire, and beyond it Berwick's wrongdoers could elude arrest by their own constables.

The lower reaches of the Tweed were not spanned again until 1820, and although the next bridge was not at Berwick but at Loan End four and a half miles upstream, it is of such interest as to merit a brief digression. For the Union Chain Bridge (54) was the first of all our suspension bridges designed to carry vehicles. Moreover, with a weight limit of two tons, it is still in use. The span is 425 feet. The designer was a seaman and engineer, Captain (later Sir Samuel) Brown. On the Scottish side − for here the Tweed has become the boundary − there is a strong stone

pylon (53) which is pierced by a comparatively small arch, with bold voussoirs; there is banded rustication throughout. On the English side the rock above the road provided adequate anchorage for the chains, so this pylon is not arched but merely built against the rockface. From the paired iron chains hangs a forest of very thin vertical bars to support the wooden road deck which since 1820 has had to be renewed three times. In recent years extensive repairs to the ironwork have also been necessary. But the original character of this graceful and historically significant bridge remains unimpaired; and now of course it is a scheduled Ancient Monument.

Back at Berwick came the next bridge across the Tweed, which still provides one of the great thrills of English railway engineering. The Royal Border Bridge (55) was designed by Robert Stephenson in 1846 and opened three years later by Queen Victoria: it was the final link in the East Coast railway line from London to Edinburgh. Two thousand men helped to build it. Its length is 2152 feet, which is just over two-fifths of a mile. There are twenty-eight arches, each with a span of $61\frac{1}{2}$ feet, but of these only twelve actually cross the water. They soar 126 feet above the bed of the Tweed. So much for the statistics: but it is other factors which grip the imagination. Artistically, the bridge gains immensely from being constructed on a sharp curve. And also from the fact that piers taper. These are of stone, while the arches are of brick and only faced with stone, as can easily be confirmed from the footpath that passes underneath. With its stately procession of round-headed arches, there is an obvious analogy with the aqueducts of Imperial Rome.

All was now well until the advent of motor traffic, for which the Old Bridge was obviously not designed. It became a notorious bottleneck; another road bridge was essential. The Royal Tweed

55. Royal Border Bridge

Bridge – Royal because for this too there was a royal opening, by the Prince of Wales – was designed and built by L. G. Mouchel and Partners between 1925 and 1928. At the time it established two records for our civil engineers: it was the longest road bridge in Britain (1410 feet) and it embodied easily the biggest reinforced concrete arch, with a span of 361 feet. (But France had already achieved several much bigger concrete spans than this.) It is 46 feet wide and leaps across the river on a rising gradient of 1 in 51; from the Tweedmouth end, in a mounting crescendo, each of its four arches rises higher and spans a greater distance than the one that precedes it (56).

How disappointing, therefore, to have to say that this is far and away the least enjoyable of these four bridges over the Tweed. Those who have written on Berwick differ only in the severity of their strictures. 'Ponderous and self-assertive', says Jack Simmons. 'A plain, vulgar graceless bullying brute', says Geoffrey Grigson. Although 'it conveys a striking impression of thrust and power', its concrete is 'chilly, stale and unsavoury looking, dirty-grey in colour and clammy in texture', says John Fleming (who at one time lived in Castlegate). There can be no doubt that, as so often nowadays, the concrete is the trouble. Only the parapets are of sandstone. The rest is naked, raw-looking concrete, which cries out for stone cladding such as was used to very good effect a few years later on London's far more elegant Waterloo Bridge. In the history of concrete engineering in this country, the Royal Tweed

56. Aerial view from the north

Bridge came at least ten years too early; at that time we were still using the material very cautiously. Had it been built today it would have been on a different system: that is, as a monolith instead of as an assembly of separate parts. The result would have been a much lighter, aesthetically more acceptable structure. Yet even those much admired concrete bridges by Maillart in Switzerland have not improved with age, as stone and brick so often do. The truth has to be faced that concrete, a marvellous material structurally, does not weather; in the course of time, even if it avoids cracking, it seldom fails to become shabby and dirty-looking.

Before long there will be yet another bridge across the Tweed, for a much-needed by-pass which is soon to be constructed. Should we be confident, or apprehensive?

Berwick's bridges are memorable, but its fortifications, in Britain, are unique. No other British towns possess defences that are in the least comparable.

A Castle was first erected here about 1150, but scarcely anything survives earlier than the time of that great castle-builder Edward I. Considerable portions of his Castle remained until 1844, when the North British Railway decided to site its railway station at just this spot. Much the same thing was done by the North Eastern Railway at Newcastle-upon-Tyne. Yet this railway vandalism was not a Northumbrian speciality: think, for instance, of Shrewsbury – and, as we shall see, Lewes. What does remain here from Edwardian times is the White Wall, dropping from the Castle ruins to the river (58). This had a narrow escape, for in 1720 workmen were prevented only at the very last moment from destroying it in order to reuse the stone for the new Barracks. One of the purposes of this wall was to protect a flight of steps – known locally as the Breakynecks! – which descends close against its inner face, from the Castle to the Water Tower on the river bank.

Otherwise there is not much to be seen now of Berwick's medieval walls. A number of other English towns — York, Chester and Chichester, in particular – can show a good deal more. With the advent of the Tudors most English towns felt that there was no longer much need for defences: but not along the Scottish border! There, on the contrary, with developments in artillery, the defences needed strengthening. Under Henry VIII a gun-tower, now ruined, was added on what is known as Lord's Mount, and the fortification of the Castle was strengthened. But these undertakings were quickly rendered obsolete by the construction, on a massive scale, of entirely new fortifications during the first eleven years of the reign of Elizabeth I (1558–69) (56).

The fortified area was now reduced by about a third. Lord's Mount was outside the protected area, so Henry VIII's gun-tower was abandoned. But the size and scale of the new fortifications are a sure indication that the English did not yet feel secure from their Northern neighbour; and about 1560 there was indeed a very real danger of another Scottish invasion, to be mounted with the help of France. The Elizabethan fortifications, much stronger than any that had existed hitherto, were constructed on quite a different plan, devised in Italy. One of the first places to use this new system was Lucca in Tuscany, in 1505, and to this day Lucca's walls (57) are even more impressive than Berwick's. Verona followed in 1523, and Antwerp in 1545. In England there was, and is, nothing at all like them.

These walls run for nearly a mile and a half. They are twenty-two feet high, twelve feet thick at the base and ten feet at the top. Basically rubble, they are faced externally with ashlared stone, which was brought from two big quarries on the cliffs nearby, both long disused. The inner faces were further strengthened by having huge quantities of earth backed up against them. The particular strength of these walls lay in the design of the bastions (56). Instead of being square or semicircular, as they would have been in the Middle Ages, they project from the walls like giant arrowheads and are connected to them by narrow 'collars'. Each bastion had a platform facing the attacker on which guns were mounted. The deep rectangular recesses formed between the bastions, the 'collars' and the main walls were called 'flankers' (59). They were also provided with guns and these fired parallel with the main walls. The guns in the 'flankers', supplementing those on the bastions, ensured that every inch of the walls was enfiladed – that is, protected by sweeping fire. A little later, by bringing up yet more earth, the tops of the bastions were heightened to enable the guns to have a longer and wider range.

57. Lucca

58. Castle ruins, White Wall and Royal Border Bridge from west

59. Brass Mount Bastion and 'Flanker'

57

58

59

60. 'Snake' seat on the Fortifications

The Elizabethan fortifications, begun in 1558, were never quite finished. When Mary Queen of Scots fled to England ten years later, one of the principal dangers was removed. With the accession of James I, they became totally redundant: in fact, a Brobdingnagian white elephant. Yet so strongly built were they that they are still extremely well preserved; and, as has been said, they are not just of local but of European importance. At least one writer on Berwick, John Fleming, has also seen in these walls 'a clean and geometric beauty', as eloquent of their purpose as they would be 'disheartening to an intending invader.*

Well, happily the invader never came. Instead, in the eighteenth century the walls became a fashionable promenade. And, in case you prefer sitting to promenading, the Victorians thoughtfully added some seats (60) supported by cast-iron snakes. Only a few of these metallic reptiles, it is sad to record, have managed to keep their tails.

But Berwick long retained its military importance. It was a garrison town, full of soldiers, which the citizens did not at all appreciate having billeted on them. So they petitioned for the erection of some barracks, and at last, in 1717–21, this was done. These were the earliest barracks to be built in Britain, and there was accommodation for nearly 600 men. The basic material is brick; over a million bricks were made just across the river at Tweedmouth, where there was abundant clay. But all the buildings were faced with the local sandstone, some of it pillaged from the Castle. The south block, within the courtyard, shows it well (61). Unluckily the flanking ranges were later cement-rendered.

These Barracks are often said to have been designed by Vanbrugh, but for this there is no documentary evidence. All that

*Those wishing to learn more about this subject should read a long article by Iain MacIvor, 'The Elizabethan Fortifications of Berwick-upon-Tweed', in *The Antiquaries Journal*, No. 45 (1965), pp. 64–96.

61–2. Barracks and Gateway

63. Holy Trinity Church

can be said with certainty is that he was in Northumberland at least once during the building period and that the style is fairly close to his. This is particularly evident in the Gateway (62), with its strong personality and touch of swagger. The Barracks are in the care of the Department of the Environment, and their future use presents something of a problem. One corner serves as a regimental museum (for the King's Own Scottish Borderers, whose regimental headquarters this was until as recently as 1965), but the south block is at present untenanted and its restoration will require considerably larger sums than are at present forthcoming.

Opposite the Barracks is a curious and unexpected building: Holy Trinity, the Parish Church (63). Unexpected because of its date, which is 1650–2; scarcely any churches were erected under the Commonwealth. Curious because of its architectural style which, outside, is an odd amalgam of classical and Gothic. An embryonic version of the so-called Venetian window, which was to become so popular in Britain in the following century, is much in evidence. A good deal of the stone is said to have been taken from the ruins of the Castle. Inside, the classical mode prevails, with an arcade borne on slender (perhaps over-slender) columns; unfortunately the stained glass (where none is needed: clear glass would be much better) is Victorian. So is the present chancel, in which, however, there is one collector's piece: a reredos, in a classical style very well suited to the church, by Lutyens. It was one of his very earliest commissions.

The large churchyard is entirely unsullied by intrusive white marble or other inappropriate kinds of stone. It is leafy, and the trees are very welcome here, in a town that is notably short of them. The chief surprise, externally, is that there is neither tower nor spire. The initiative for raising the money needed to replace the small, indifferent medieval parish church by the present building came from Colonel George Fenwick, who was Governor of Berwick and a friend of Cromwell; and it is always said, although there are no documents to support it, that it was at the Protector's special request that no tower was added, because of his antipathy to bells. Even today that is symbolic of something very close to the heart of Berwick: its puritanism. This is a town in which Nonconformity had always flourished. John Knox had arrived here to preach in 1549 and had stayed two years. John Wesley came first in 1748 and returned no fewer than eighteen times. After 1759 he usually preached in the Town Hall, presumably because none of the numerous meeting houses was large enough to accommodate his congregation.

64. Town Hall

65. 'Justice' in Council Chamber, Town Hall

When at length Holy Trinity did acquire a set of bells, they were hung not in its own tower, for none was ever built, but in that of the Town Hall (64). This dates from the 1750s. With its somewhat pinched proportions it is certainly no masterpiece, but it is without doubt the most prominent building in Berwick, and right in the centre of the old walled town. Its sandstone came from two quarries, New Mills and Edrington, three and four miles to the west. The octagonal cupola, crowned by a short spire, is the chief feature of Berwick's skyline. It is just 150 feet to the gilded weathervane. From the open gallery above the cupola, accessible only by somewhat perilous ladders, there are big views in every direction. The bellringers' chamber is furnished with a row of glass beer mugs, accompanied by this admonition:

> Keep stroak of time and goe not out
> Or elles you forfeit out of doubt
> For every fault a jugge of beer.

But no longer is the chime of eight bells rung for the Church. One of them, however, seems to have been sounded during the eighteenth century to apprise the garrison and the townsfolk of the opening and closing of the town gates. In the following century the early morning bell was discontinued because of its unpopularity with the slumbering citizens; but except on Sundays the curfew bell, powered now by an electric motor, is still rung each evening between 8.00 and 8.15: just one example among many, in England, of the survival of a harmless anachronism.

The top floor of the main building once housed the Town Gaol. It is now open to the public. It must have been an abode of misery.

The various categories of prisoner were kept separate. One cell was for female wrongdoers. They had a straw mattress, on which up to four women could sleep side by side. If there were more than four, the others had to sleep on the floor or take it in turns. The rougher characters might be confined in leg-irons. Top security prisoners had their own separate cell, a veritable cage; and so did drunks. But the grimmest place is the cell for those condemned to die. The last occupant was Grace Griffin, who was convicted in 1823 for the murder of her husband. Although protesting her innocence to the last, she was led off hence to the gallows, on the hill just beyond the Castle.

On the floor below, the first floor, is a pleasant Georgian room, now the Council Chamber, with a plaster relief of Justice (65) by Joseph Alexander (for which he was paid £5!). She is blindfolded, as a symbol of the Law's impartiality, and set within a pretty Rococo cartouche. Originally the background within this frame was Wedgwood blue, and it would not be difficult to restore this. The figure would be much more effective against a blue background.

These, then, are Berwick's principal buildings; what now of the general aspect of the town? I cannot improve on the verdict of Sir Nikolaus Pevsner: 'a fine town, with closed street walls, houses not in themselves of great architectural merit, but blending well with each other and with the fortifications and the sea.' Its hilliness is also visually a great asset. And although Edward I's liking for chequerboard plans, well seen at Winchelsea in Sussex, was not therefore feasible here, a certain regularity can still be detected (51).

Mr Francis Cowe, Berwick's local historian,* has drawn attention to the association of the medieval streets with particular trades, something which is still quite common in the cities of the Orient. Woolmarket, behind the Town Hall, speaks for itself; here was the former Wool Pack Inn. Walkergate is less obvious; this was the abode of the fullers or dressers of cloth, who washed it by 'walking' it through water. (We shall find exactly the same thing at Beverley; see page 180.) Church Street was formerly Sutergate, the street of the shoemakers. Silver Street used to be called Hidegate, and may well have been the street of the leather workers. Incidentally, Berwick has several other streets with names ending in 'gate': Marygate, Castlegate, Sandgate. This suffix is common all over North-Eastern England, and I often used to wonder why. It has no connection with gating. It is simply the English form of the old Norse word *gata*, meaning a road or street.

By 1603, Berwick was no more than a poor garrison town. With the Scottish King's accession to the throne of England, its recovery began, but proceeded only very slowly until the Act of Union of 1707. This was a landmark in the town's history, for it meant that normal trade with the Scottish hinterland could at last be resumed.

*Berwick-upon-Tweed: *A Short Historical Guide* by F. M. Cowe (1975) is warmly recommended. It is published by Bell's Bookshop, Marygate, Berwick.

66. Pantiles

1750–1850 was the century of Berwick's greatest prosperity. Within the walls there was now some overcrowding. That is why a few of the houses are in courts, built on what were once gardens, and approached along passages which may start by burrowing under main street houses.

During the 'prosperous century' the old town was largely rebuilt, in carefully masoned stone. Quarries in the vicinity were numerous: several have already been mentioned. Sometimes, it is true, the stone was only employed, as it had been at the Barracks, as a facing for brick, but this was a perfectly legitimate and sensible practice, followed in all England's stone districts at this time. The stone used, as throughout the whole area of the lower Tweed, was a calciferous sandstone, somewhat pink in its pristine state but often decidedly dour after long exposure to the weather. Since 1970 a good deal of this stonework has been cleaned, and, apart altogether from questions of preservation (more applicable to limestones than to sandstones), there can as a general rule be little doubt that stone is visually much improved by cleaning: limestones almost always are. But with the sandstones of Berwick it has to be granted that there are losses as well as gains. The somewhat bland aspect of the cleaned houses in Ravensdowne (68) and Wellington Terrace (74) contrasts with the undeniably more interesting texture of those which have so far been left untouched. In the case of a terrace it really should be all or none, by mutual agreement between the owners.

Until the eighteenth century most of Berwick's roofs would have been of thatch, of which not a single example survives. Nearly all the Georgian and Victorian roofs are either pantiles or slates (67).

'Pantiles', observes John Cornforth, 'are as important in Berwick as Collyweston roofs are in Stamford.'* They are considerably bigger than plain tiles and, being made roughly in the shape of a flattened S, they are able to overlap not only in a downward direction but also transversally, the down-bent edge of one tile hooking over the upturned edge of its neighbour. Their wavy surface gives them a delightful texture and surface richness (66): red pantiles are indeed one of the most enjoyable sights of eastern and north-eastern England. They only became available at the end of the seventeenth century, at first by being brought from Holland, perhaps as ballast, in ships which on the outward voyage had carried our coal and other products. But from about 1760 most of them came from Cocklaw, about two and a half miles to the west, and by 1800 from numerous other tileworks in the neighbourhood. Today they have to be obtained from Hull, which often involves long delays. But great emphasis is rightly placed on using them wherever possible and, in particular, on retaining those that are already there. Other modern tiles, often machine-made and sometimes of concrete, are very much inferior.

The other principal roofing material is slate, no longer easily obtainable here. Several kinds were used. The most pleasing are

*His three excellent articles on Berwick appeared in *Country Life* in April–May 1980.

67. View from Town Hall cupola, looking north-east

68. 2–16 Ravensdowne

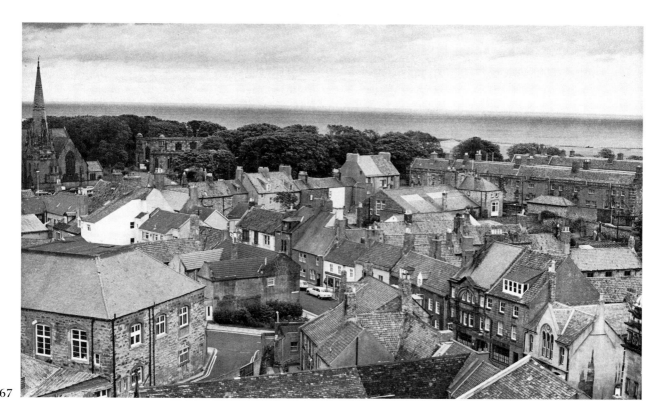

67

68

69. Cowport

71. 4–5 Quay Walls

70. 37 Woolmarket

the grey-blue and grey-green Westmorland and Cumberland slates, with which the town is well provided. Others, mostly of nineteenth-century date, include very dark Scottish slate from Ballahulish, purplish Welsh slate from Portmadoc, and even some from Norway.

The handling of stone at Berwick is a constant source of interest and pleasure. The contrast between rubblestone and freestone is well illustrated in the view of Cowport (69). The little building on the left, the Gatekeeper's Lodge, built in 1755, is ashlared, and ashlar can only be achieved with freestone: stone, that is, with enough homogeneity of structure and fineness of grain to admit of being hewn 'freely', with the aid of a saw, into carefully squared, and often quite large smooth-faced blocks. The Berwick sandstones have this property, so the standard of masonry here is almost uniformly good.

What, however, is surprising is to find that so much of the stonework has been tooled. Lightly tooled surfaces, in a variety of patterns, are something of a Berwick speciality. Woolmarket (70) has an extraordinary display: there is hardly a house which does not show it. I can only account for it in terms of a local fashion.

Plenty more can be seen along one of Berwick's most enjoyable streets, Quay Walls, which is for walkers only. Some valiant work of restoration has been accomplished here during the last few years. Two examples are Nos 4 and 5 (71), both originally dating from the latter part of the eighteenth century. No. 5, the house in the foreground, is one of a group lately saved from near-dereliction and brought back to life by the local Preservation Trust, which has done, and is doing, a splendid job in this town.

72. 18 Quay Walls, the Custom House

At the Custom House, No. 18 (72), where the sandstone has also been cleaned, the restoration was Government-sponsored. This gracious little building is somewhat Adam-like in character, with an exceptionally attractive fanlight over the door and, to either side of it, pairs of fluted Tuscan pilasters.

At the Lions House (73), another excellent example of sandstone ashlar, the surface is not tooled. This is one of the tallest houses in Berwick, and the most strikingly situated. It stands alone in an extremely exposed situation close to the Elizabethan walls, and facing directly into the bitterly cold east winds which sometimes blow in off the North Sea. It is therefore perfectly appropriate that, except for the quoins, the front should be almost devoid of adornment. As so often with Georgian architecture, it is on the subtlety of the proportions that its impact depends. It will be noticed how at each storey the size of the windows is quietly reduced. A few years ago this house fell into such bad condition that it was in danger of being demolished. But first the Preservation Trust

73. Lions House, Windmill Hill

stepped in, and then two local businessmen heroically undertook the work of restoration. Putting back all the missing glazing bars into the windows effected a veritable transformation in the appearance of the building. And here there can be no question of the effectiveness of the cleaned stonework.

For siting, the Lions House has at Berwick only one rival, which is Wellington Terrace (74), a group of three houses looking nearly due south across the Tweed estuary. The middle one has been cleaned, and again I have to say that it would have been better to have cleaned all or none. Where one's house is part of a terrace, individual initiative really does need to be disciplined. The dormers of No. 1 are an inept addition, but still worse is the reglazing of all the windows of No. 3 (happily, perhaps, not visible in the photograph). Each house was intended to have its portico; unfortunately, the central one was later demolished and the third one never built. On the other hand, the blank windows on the side wall of No. 1 are good: they were introduced to articulate

74. 1–3 Wellington Terrace

ornamentally what would otherwise have been an uninteresting expanse of plain wall. Needless to say, they have nothing to do with the Window Tax.

In Castlegate there is a terrace of ten houses. No. 1 (75), dated 1849, is very similar to the middle house in Wellington Terrace but has not been cleaned. How much better it is than the corresponding house at the other end of the terrace (76). Quite apart from the mutilation of the ground floor windows, the painting of the stonework here, with the rest of the long terrace unpainted, can only be described as an architectural solecism.

For painting or colour-washing a house can completely transform its character. Where the masonry is good, this may be aesthetically a very questionable practice. Nonetheless, Berwick has a good many examples. I select three hotels, and it must, I feel, be concluded that if stonework is to be painted, white makes the best livery for the wall, with other colours confined to the dressings. At the Ravensholme (79) the stone has been stuccoed and painted khaki; at the King's Arms (77), with its naïve but rather endearing proliferation of Venetian windows in two different sizes, the dressings are cocoa-brown; at the Bridge Hotel (78) grey-brown, which is undeniably elegant, and certainly justified here if, like the exposed side elevation, the wall was only rubblestone.

This is an unusual front, full of character. The central feature consists of a tetrastyle portico (a term derived from Greek and meaning four columns across) set above a broad flight of steps

75. 1 Castlegate

76. 19 Castlegate

75

76

77

78

leading to a pretty doorcase flanked by niches, with upstairs another Venetian window, surmounted here by a pediment. With slender glazing bars adorning all the windows, and a roof of new but richly textured pantiles, this house, which not many years ago was smothered in ivy, seems to me a model of good restoration.

It is in truth about the only building of distinction in Tweedmouth, the home of the Twempies, as the people there are called by the Berwickers! Although on the other side of the river, it was within the former borough. As it is very prominently sited, facing directly across the Old Bridge, the good appearance of this little hotel matters enormously.

The scene at the Berwick end of the Old Bridge is architecturally more confused, but in 1938 provided the subject for a characteristic painting by L. S. Lowry (80) which in 1975 was unhappily stolen; its present whereabouts are unknown.

Architecturally it was fortunate for Berwick that its most prosperous period was when the Classical style was in the ascendant. A small but interesting military survivor is the Old Guard House (81), with another tetrastyle portico and pediment. This was first erected during the eighteenth century in Marygate. By 1815 it was no longer needed by the Army, so in that year it was moved stone by stone to its present site close to Palace Green: surely a very early example of careful preservation.

But preservation does pose great problems at Berwick. Besides the walls and the Barracks, there is the old and now wholly abandoned shipyard below Quay Walls which is in the foreground of many of the town's best views. A few of the buildings here are acceptable: others are frankly eyesores and cry out for removal.

81. Old Guard House, Palace Green

Farther east, in Pier Road, there is a good example of how the old malt houses can be converted to a new use (84). They are now occupied by a firm that manufactures marquees and tents, sails and tarpaulins.

The harbour was long a source of prosperity. In the Middle Ages it was from here that large quantities of Cheviot and Border wool were shipped abroad. Later came the products of the rich Tweed-basin farmland: corn, beef-cattle, hides, butter and eggs. Plenty of fish, too, especially salmon, a delicacy which can still be enjoyed here at not too exorbitant a price. There was also sea-fishing. Today the harbour is quiet, but not moribund. It is still used by perhaps 150 small merchant ships (of up to about a thousand tons burthen a year, as well as by fishing boats and pleasure craft. The chief imports are fertilisers; the principal export is barley, which may be sold as far away as Poland.

The grain is still dried and stored in a few of the big granaries, with sloping walls and lichen-clad roofs, which were put up in the later eighteenth century on the landward side of the Quay Walls (83). The access lanes pass underneath the walls to reach the quay. These granaries, early monuments of 'industrial archaeology', constitute yet another problem of preservation. One is now a store; several are untenanted; others have already been demolished. Since the last war huge modern granaries and malt-houses have been built on the new trading estate in Tweedmouth, and most of this type of business is now operated from there.

Paradoxically the coming of the railway, and the opening of the Royal Border Bridge, did not help Berwick. For the produce of the Tweed no longer had to travel by ship to find its markets. So by 1875, when the classical style of architecture was quite out of favour, Murray's *Handbook for Travellers in Scotland* wrote of Berwick: 'The town is best seen from the railway and is not worth entering'.

For a while, it is true, this town did undeniably look rather down-at-heel. Buildings as handsome as the former Governor's House (82) on Palace Green, erected early in the eighteenth century and even attributed, improbably enough, to Vanbrugh,

82. Governor's House, Palace Green

83. Old Granaries, Dewars Lane

84. Old Malt House

82

83

84

were treated with ruthless disrespect. But since the formation in 1971 of the Berwick Town Preservation Trust, a veritable transformation has taken place. Berwick is also one of the places which has responded to the encouragement offered by the Historic Buildings Council for England to set up what is known as a Town Scheme. Under this, any sums allocated to restoration or preservation by the local authorities, maybe with help from their County Council, are doubled by the Department of the Environment. In the section of Quay Walls here illustrated (85), every single house – apart from the Custom House on the extreme left, which was referred to earlier – received some assistance between 1976 and 1980, and the visual benefit has been remarkable.

The object of these offers of financial help is to provide owners of both residential and commercial property with an incentive to invest in their own towns, and to persuade local authorities to become committed to programmes of repairs. Even items such as street lamps are not overlooked. Quay Walls has some new ones which were a contribution to European Architectural Heritage Year (1975).

Despite its fine situation, no one, I think, could claim that Berwick is a seductive town. What it has is character: strong character. And two features which are, in England, unique; its fortifications and its bridges. It seems certain that for much of its future prosperity it must now look to tourism. In this direction both the town and its surroundings have much to offer.

Berwick is small and not at all rich; and with so many old buildings, not all with any obvious use today, preservation here is a daunting undertaking. All honour, then, to this sturdy little town for having taken up the challenge so gallantly.

85. 19–22 Quay Walls

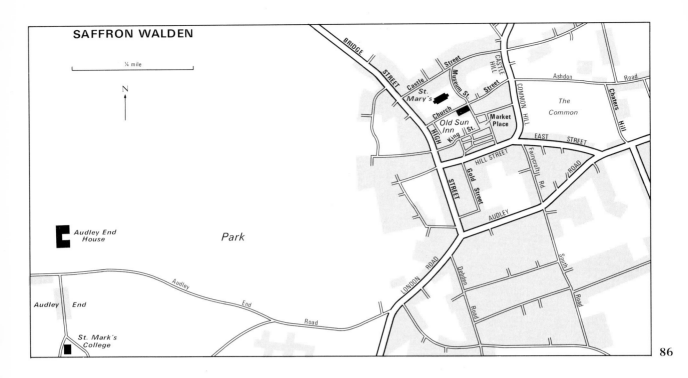

SAFFRON WALDEN

¼ mile

N

Audley End House

Park

Audley End

St. Mark's College

BRIDGE STREET
Castle Street
Museum St.
CASTLE HILL
St. Mary's Church
Street
Old Sun Inn
HIGH STREET
King St.
Market Place
COMMON HILL
Ashdon Road
Chaters Hill
The Common
EAST STREET
Farncroft Rd.
ROAD
AUDLEY
HILL STREET
Gold Street
STREET
LONDON ROAD
Debden Road
South Road

86

87. View of Church and Town from the North

3. Saffron Walden

Nearly thirty years ago, the Folk-Lore Society (I am not making this up: you can find them in the London Telephone Directory) solemnly affirmed that the British people who believed in fairies less than any others were the inhabitants of Essex. Belief in fairies, their report went on to say, is usually most developed in districts with a suitably picturesque landscape and among races with an imaginative mentality and a love of legend: 'none of these conditions holds in Essex'. And it is certainly true that the rest of England does not regard Essex as picturesque. Yet away from the commuter belt the county has, in addition to some memorably attractive villages, many tracts of countryside notable for their quiet pastoral calm. This is particularly true of its north-western corner, where the principal place is Saffron Walden.

All this part of Essex used to be densely wooded. But there is evidence that Bronze and Iron Ages tribes, following the River Cam, settled in this area: Ring Hill, a mile and a half to the west of the present town, was an Iron Age fort. The Romans came here too, and so did the Saxons, but evidence of any pre-Norman buildings is virtually non-existent. The Normans cleared away much of the woodland around the town, and rebuilt in stone the wooden church and castle of the Saxons. The church, as we shall see, was entirely rebuilt again.

The Castle did not function for long; it was already in decay by the middle of the thirteenth century. It was built of flint, and all that survives today are some sizeable fragments of the twelfth-century keep. Like nearly all flint ruins they are amorphous and wholly unpicturesque.

The powerful family here in Norman times were the de Mandevilles, and about 1140, a mile or so west of the town near the present site of Audley End House, Geoffrey de Mandeville founded a Benedictine Priory, which fifty years later attained the status of an Abbey. It was from the monks that in 1295 the town was granted the right to hold a market every Tuesday.

Not later than the fourteenth century the original settlement of Walden became known as Chipping (Chepying) Walden. Several other English towns and villages still retain this prefix: Chipping Campden, Chipping Norton, Chipping Warden, Chipping Sodbury. High Barnet was formerly Chipping Barnet, and Ongar Chipping Ongar. It means market; and is derived from the Anglo-Saxon word 'to buy', from which also comes Cheapside in the City of London.

A market town it was then, and so it is still. A general market is held every Tuesday and Saturday, and on Saturdays there is a cattle market as well. There is good soil in every direction, so for many of the smallholders this is the focal point. As at Berwick, the medieval street pattern, based upon trade, survives (86). There were Butchers' Row, Mercers' Row, Tanners' Row, Fish Row, the Butter Market and Pig Street, which was the swine market. The

88. *Crocus sativus*

89. Saffron Walden's coat of arms

erstwhile traders left these narrow streets long ago, but the names recall the time when every street had its own trade.

The market place itself came somewhat later, when people wanted, once every week, to have space to set up their stalls; in the eighteenth century this had to be enlarged. The trade here was mainly in agricultural produce. But, as so often in England in the Middle Ages, the town's chief source of wealth was wool. It was principally the wool merchants who paid for the lavish rebuilding of the parish church near the end of the Gothic age.

Not long after this – in the early Tudor period – Chipping Walden began to be called Saffron Walden; and the explanation is again bound up with trade. Improbably, it might be thought, for the saffron is a crocus. *Crocus sativus* is a native of Kashmir and of the Near East. It was known to the ancient Greeks and Romans and also to the Arabs: indeed, the name derives from the Arabic word *Za-faran.* It was first brought into England during the reign of Edward III. By the middle of the fifteenth century it was being grown extensively, but the bulbs will only flower in a calcareous soil, and not always then. It was tried in Suffolk and Norfolk, and also in Gloucestershire, but not nearly so successfully as here. It was just in this small area of north-west Essex and the adjoining strip of Cambridgeshire that it became commercially important.

The graceful mauve flowers start blooming towards the end of October. The valuable part of the flower (88) was the long vermilion stigmas, which each autumn were carefully collected, dried, and pressed into blocks for convenient transport or storage, To be ready for use, a block had to be soaked overnight. Over 4000 flowers were needed to produce just one ounce of the finished product, so it was always expensive. Its primary use was as a dye: the red stigmas produced not a red but a yellow dye. It was probably the local clothiers who first encouraged this cultivation; by 1500 a representation of it could already be seen – and still can – high up in the south arcade of the church. But it was also used in cooking, for flavouring, and medicinally – as an antidote, it was believed, to the plague, and as a remedy for pimples; and if you took an overdose it could leave you helpless with laughter for hours on end. Very inconvenient!

It was cultivated so intensively in many of the fields round about that in autumn they became a sea of mauve. So important did this industry become that by the middle of the sixteenth century the saffron crocus figured on the coat of arms (89), which may well have been the reason for the change in the town's name. Throughout the Tudor and Stuart periods the trade flourished. Presents of saffron were given by the Corporation to many distinguished visitors, among them James I, Charles I, and George I. Its fame was recorded by John Evelyn in his Diary when he visited Audley End in 1654: 'that fine palace . . . is in Saffron Walden parish, famous for that useful plant, with which all the country is covered'.

And then, quite early in the eighteenth century, cultivation of *Crocus sativus* suddenly ceased. Its efficacy in medicine was being

90. Youth Hostel, 1–3 Bridge Street, Myddleton Place elevation

questioned. Cheaper yellow dyes were discovered. And in the kitchen it survived into the present century for no more than the occasional flavouring of cakes and biscuits, for which purpose it now has to be imported, mainly from Spain. It is only quite recently that this strain of crocus has been recovered and replanted here on a small scale, thanks to the initiative of a body of public-spirited townspeople. Happily, however, since the sixteenth century Walden has never shed its Saffron!*

Saffron was replaced by malt. The former crocus fields were sown with barley. By the beginning of the nineteenth century this town was one of the three most important in Essex for malting. It was also a stronghold of nonconformity, and especially of the Quakers, who are often total abstainers. But the wealthy Gibson family, who lived at 7 High Street (118), had no such inhibitions. They had their maltings next door.

Close by is the town's leading example of timber-framing, 1–3 Bridge Street. A prominent feature of the long side-elevation in Myddleton Place (90) is the sack hoist which was added when this ancient house was converted into a malting. The building, with a jettied upper storey, goes back to the end of the fifteenth century. Of special interest are the pair of small, four-light oriel windows with

*For much interesting information about the saffron crocus, I have been indebted to an unpublished study (1973) by Mr H. C. Stacey, the former Town Clerk, and to the Saffron Walden Museum Leaflet No. 13 (1980), by Mrs J. A. Hirsh.

91. Dormitory, Youth Hostel

92. 32 High Street

93. 18–20 High Street

94. 4 High Street

91

92

93

94

moulded sills. Their original oak is still in excellent condition.

The upper room (91), in which can still be seen, up in the roof, the oak wheel of the maltster's hoist, is now the dormitory of Saffron Walden's Youth Hostel. What a thrilling experience it must be to wake up under this splendid double-framed oak roof, with ties, collars, braces and studs – the whole hosier's shop, in fact! The studs are the vertical timbers; braces are the curved pieces which run along the full length of the room below the purlins, securing the structure longitudinally, as the tie and collar beams do crosswise.

The Youth Hostels Association, now over fifty years old, has established some of its hostels in buildings of considerable architectural and historic merit. Indeed, no fewer than six, including a college (Thoresby College at King's Lynn), an Elizabethan manor house (Wilderhope Manor, Shropshire) and a couple of castles (Pendennis in Cornwall and St Briavels in Gloucestershire), as well as this house, are scheduled Grade One by the Department of the Environment.

Essex is a county very poorly off for building stone, so for centuries all its houses were timber-framed and thatched. Towards the end of the Middle Ages the cruder wattle and daub infilling gave way to the more refined lath and plaster, but the oak framework did not change. What did change was the external finish: in this part of England many of the houses were completely plastered over, including some, like the Youth Hostel or 44–46 High Street (95), the timbers of which had originally been exposed.

95. 44–46 High Street

The plastering was done partly for comfort; it had the effect of excluding at least some of the draughts to which, as anyone who has ever lived in a timber-framed house will know, such buildings are by no means inaccessible! But from the middle of the seventeenth-century it was also done for appearance. It was now felt to be better manners not to reveal the bones below the skin, as it were. Saffron Walden abounds in timber-framed houses wearing plaster overcoats, some well-tailored and of smart appearance, as at 44–46 High Street, others decidedly home-spun and with no aspirations to smartness, like 33 Bridge Street (96).

In the present century there has been a great vogue for exposed timbers, so much so in fact that speculative builders on suburban housing estates, as is well known, were commonly (and that is the right word) addicted to fixing strips of wood, particularly on to the fronts of upper storeys and gables, to simulate timber-framing where it did not and could not possibly exist. (In recent years improvements in taste, abetted by the sharp rise in the cost of wood, have fortunately brought this practice to an end.) In accordance with this fashion for exposed wood, a great deal of plaster has been stripped away from timber-framed buildings. 4 (94) and 18–20 (93) High Street are but two examples in Saffron Walden.

I do not want to deny that exposed oak timbers can be very attractive; of course they can. But once they have been plastered over, laths will have been nailed on to provide a key. Remove these, and it will be found that the oak studs are pitted with nail holes

96. 33 Bridge Street

97. Saffron Hotel, 6–12 High Street

which can prove very unsightly. Yet the stripping away of old plaster still goes on, if less frequently than a generation ago.

What is specially wrong is to strip and then to blacken, as at 32 High Street (92), a building which has been drastically reconstructed more than once. Black and white, as observed earlier, is a West country affair, and anyway is mostly Victorian. It has no place in Essex. In my view it is also a cruel way of treating oak, which is such a beautiful wood in its natural state.

But if the plaster on a timber-framed building is retained, there is much to be said for colouring it, and in this respect we have in recent years done well. Several excellent products are now available in a wide range of colours, of which people in Saffron Walden have taken full advantage. The Saffron Hotel (97), appropriately enough, is yellow.

The plaster might also be rendered more interesting by the addition of pargeting, which has long been especially characteristic of north-west Essex and south-west Suffolk. Put simply, what is meant by pargeting (which can also be spelt 'pargetting') is the application of patterns on to wet plaster. In olden days the plaster was all lime-based. Today it varies. A good mixture in current use is six parts sand to two parts lime to one part Portland cement.

Pargeting can be done in two ways. Nowadays almost all of it is incised – that is to say, pressed in – while the plaster is still wet. This may be done by means of a wooden mould, usually now made of deal, or with a tool called a comb. In this kind of pargeting the designs are usually mildly geometrical and can be delightful (100). Unfortunately others can look very mechanical (98). Incised pargeting has a long history, but what we see today has practically always been renewed.

98. Incised pargeting at 23 Castle Street

99. 6 Gold Street

Pargeting in relief is a much more ambitious and interesting process. The heyday of this craft, in Saffron Walden as elsewhere, was the seventeenth century. Also done while the plaster was still wet, these designs might be impressed from moulds too, which were occasionally of beeswax but usually wood; but often they were just modelled freehand with the fingers, aided by a few small tools. The gilded panel with the dolphin on the front of 6 Gold Street (99) was brought here from the former inn of that name in the Market Place.

Where, as here, there is a jetty (or overhang), there will be a fascia-board masking the ends of the upper floor-boards. This was a favourite place for pargeting; below the panel is what is called a trail, also with the dolphin motif, for which two moulds were used alternately. Sometimes, as at 18–20 High Street (93), the pargeting will be on the face of the summer, the massive horizontal beam that supports the joists of the upper floor, which may or may not project: here it does. This parget-work, again impressed from moulds, consists of swags and foliage. Sometimes, on summers and fascia-boards, there is no more than a simple wavy pattern, modelled by hand. Unfortunately the horizontal surfaces of this relief pargeting are all too prone to collect dirt, which mars the effect. They should receive the constant attention of a duster or a damp cloth.

Saffron Walden has one showpiece of seventeenth-century

100. Pargeting at 10 Castle Street

101. Old Sun Inn, Church Street

102. Old Sun Inn

pargeting, on the front of the former Sun Inn in Church Street (101), most of which is said, by the man who was responsible for restoration work here in 1966, to be original. The most striking group is that over the carriageway entrance (2). Here are the rude figures of two men in seventeenth-century clothes. The one on the right, with the club, is reputed to be the Wisbech Giant. The other, with raised sword, is said to represent Tom Hickathrift, who in his day was a well-known East Anglian carter. Between them is a large cartwheel, with the spokes now only faintly visible. The Giant's legs had to be completely renewed in 1966. They were modelled by hand in hair-lime plaster, just as in the seventeenth century, and the work was so well done that nobody would realise that it was not original.

Next comes a stocking, which suggests that this building, or at least this room, was used at one time as a hosiery. Then, to the left of the three-light upstairs window, there is a pretty but fairly conventional design of birds, fishes and foliage in facing pairs (104). After that come two elaborately ornamented gables, both with birds and foliage and the first (103) with crude bunches of fruit in addition, together with a pair of big straps and a simple interlaced arcade. On the farther gable (102) is an oval cartouche with the date 1676. No one could pretend that this is anything more than folk art; but as such, it is rather delightful, and an exceptionally complete survival.

The framework of all these houses, pargeted or not, is oak. This wonderful wood is never far from our thoughts, nor indeed from our eyes, at Saffron Walden. But not many places can show Tudor shop windows, as can be seen here in Cross Street, a narrow turning off King Street. There are two of them, facing each other. Both, it must be said, have been a good deal restored, and originally of course they were unglazed. The better one (106), although now hiding under a coat of white paint, still keeps its moulded jambs, characteristically Tudor four-centred arches, and carving in the spandrels.

Another use of wood was for weather-boarding. This, which is usually soft wood, and scarcely ever oak, appeared in England a good deal later than framed structures, and is not common at Saffron Walden. The best example is a barn (105), and for barns the boards were traditionally tarred.

This barn at 22 Bridge Street is also notable for the beautiful hand-made tiles of its roof. Only a quarter of the original number survive: the farther end has Welsh slate and at the back the corrugated iron is a lot worse, but there is a fine uninterrupted stretch. And elsewhere in the town there are still plenty of old tiles, the rich colours and textures of which are a continual source of pleasure (109). They are all plain tiles here: pantiles are exceptional in Essex.

Because of the dearth of stone, Essex was also one of the first English counties to adopt brick as a regular building material. By Henry VIII's time entire churches were being built of it, as well as some memorable houses. For owners of timber-framed houses, the special value of brick, being fire-resistant, was for chimneys, and it is not without significance that the earliest brickwork at Saffron Walden, probably Elizabethan, is a group of four lofty octagonal chimneys at 17 Bridge Street (107) which rise from moulded bases and are linked at the top. There is one other, in Audley End village, which is a mile away but still within the parish. Abbey House was much altered in the eighteenth century and again recently, but some of the original chimneys survive (108); and several of these are

103–104. Old Sun Inn

106. Tudor shop windows, Cross Street

105. Barn, 22 Bridge Street

107. Chimneys, 17 Bridge Street

108. Abbey House, Audley End Village

adorned with raised designs, specially made piece by piece in moulds and fitted together as the stack went up: a glorious extravagance, more characteristic of the reign of Henry VIII than that of his daughter.

Nearly all the best brickwork, however, is Georgian. It may only be skin deep. 6 Church Street started life in the fifteenth century as a normal timber-framed building. It was altered in the sixteenth and again in the seventeenth centuries, and on the garden side (111) it still retains a trio of gables. Then in the eighteenth century it was given a gracious new Georgian street front (110), hiding, needless to say, every trace of its wooden origin. Nor is this by any means an unique example here. It was so much less expensive than pulling down one's house and building anew, and few people could afford to do this anyway, even if they wanted to.

37 High Street (112), now the Post Office, was originally a seventeenth-century house, refronted in the Georgian period and later very much altered. The French windows above the door are a great pity; they were inserted when a first-floor balcony was added. This has since been removed, and it would be good to see the original window restored. Still, it is a handsome building, with some beautiful brick craftsmanship. Particularly pleasing are the quoins of the projecting centrepiece. They are composed of specially soft bricks known as 'rubbers', since they could be rubbed down in order to achieve the finest possible joint. Here they were chamfered to achieve the sort of rusticated effect which was normal at this time if building in stone. Rather surprisingly, considering the date, the front is built with English bond: that is to say, with the bricks laid in alternating courses of all headers and all stretchers. By this date the usual bond was what is called Flemish,

109. 41–43 Castle Street

110. 6 Church Street, front

111. 6 Church Street, from the garden

109

110

111

112. The Post Office, 37 High Street

although it is seldom seen in Flanders: that is, with every course consisting of alternating headers and stretchers.

72 High Street (115) also dates from the seventeenth century; the prominent chimney-stack, although much rebuilt, is of that date. But the house was remodelled in the Georgian era, and the canted bays, with their ugly windows, are of course Victorian. Hiding under a Virginia creeper which certainly has no business to be here is another excellent example of brick craftsmanship. In so far as it is possible to see them, there are, again, the quoins, and a very elaborately wrought surround to the door, with rusticated brick pilasters.

At the Conservative Club, 3 Museum Street (113), we can see how canted bays should be glazed on a Georgian front. And this building is also interesting as an example of that curious super-refinement of Georgian brickwork known as tuck-pointing. Of this Saffron Walden has a number of examples.

By the addition of sand of the right colour and perhaps an oxide, a mortar could be produced which matched almost exactly the colour of the bricks. (In the example illustrated (114) the match is not nearly as good as it should be.) With this mortar the joints would be pointed absolutely flush with the wall surface. Then, while still damp, these mortar joints would be scored with narrow grooves not more than an eighth of an inch wide, into which would be pressed thin ribbons of a contrasting colour: generally, as here, white chalk-lime putty. The object was to obtain an effect of very fine jointing less expensively than by using all rubbers, but it was still not cheap and certainly not as durable.

114. Tuck pointing, 37 High Street

113. 3–5 Museum Street

115. 72 High Street

There were several brickworks in the neighbourhood of Saffron Walden, notably at Ashdon, four miles to the north-east. At one time there were also brick kilns in Audley End Park, which was still nearer. In the first half of the nineteenth century red brick was rather out of fashion, and at this time there was a liking, here as elsewhere, for Gault bricks, made from chalky clay – of which there was plenty round about – with little or no iron in it to stain it red. 1 and 2 Chaters Hill (116), built in the 1830s, are a typical example. It is a very sober-sided material: often indeed somewhat drab.

At Saffron Walden people would seem not infrequently to have become bored with Gault bricks (as I do) and to have painted them. The junction of Church Street and High Street is now alive with pinks and yellows: the most distinguished building here is The Pump House (117), which is attired in salmon pink! These people, despite their Quaker inheritance, evidently love colour – I commented earlier on the colouring of plaster over timber-framing – and good luck to them, I say.

Generally, though, if a painted surface is required, as in the first half of the nineteenth century it so often was, and as nowadays it

116. 1–2 Chaters Hill

117. The Pump House, 14 High Street

often is again, stucco (hard plaster) undoubtedly provides a more urbane finish. Three examples are illustrated here: all on the west side of the High Street. All are brick houses, 7 and 73 Georgian in origin. Number 73 (119), with a very elegant fanlight over the door, is the most original, especially at first-floor level: the parapet is also unusual and the keystones are a feature throughout. Number 7 (118) was formerly the house of the Gibson family, referred to earlier. The facing of a Georgian red brick house with stucco – and even the rusticated quoins are of this material – was no doubt their doing. Number 53 (120) is a Regency house which was stuccoed from the time that it was built. It has the wide eaves and low-pitched roof typical of the period, but the ground floor is quite unusual; instead of the canted bays with three windows seen at No. 7 and at 3 Museum Street, there are bows with only two windows, set in arched recesses. Stucco needs to be well maintained. When, as at all these three houses, it is, the town benefits greatly.

Saffron Walden is well endowed with trees, which figure prominently in many of the views (87): and a great asset they are. Yet in the upper part of the High Street they do present something of a problem (121). The street widens out, but not by any means sufficiently to accommodate London planes, one of the varieties which were planted here in 1902. Having grown too big for comfort, these unhappy trees are subjected, every year, to drastic

120. 53 High Street

121. The High Street, looking north

122. Swan Lodge

pollarding in the French manner. So in the winter months their poor mutilated trunks are not only no asset but really something of an eyesore. Welcome as trees so often are in towns, anything like an avenue of large trees is a very doubtful amenity unless the street is really very wide indeed. The alternative would seem to be to plant only very small trees in this kind of situation, and to some extent this is what has more recently been done. Elsewhere, of course, the incidence of trees can be a lovely complement to the architecture: but they must never be allowed to overpower it. Nor, let me add, to vulgarise it, as can so easily be done with, say, a row of pink-flowering cherries.

Among the smaller buildings of Saffron Walden, which means nearly all the buildings, for this friendly little town has never harboured any 'monumental' ambitions, stone is only notable for its absence. The one exception is flint, which is also rare, but how good it can look is well seen at Swan Lodge (122), which used to be one of the entrance lodges to Audley End Park. This is an early Victorian flint building with brick dressings.

But the place to see flint in quantity is the Church – and a pretty nondescript impression it makes there, with lumps of clunch (which is chalk) and odd bits of brick mixed in. The masonry of the lowest stage of the tower is equally crude, but as our eyes move upwards, they meet something very different: fine-quality limestone (123). This is, surprisingly enough, Monk's Park oolite, one of the Bath stones, quarried near Corsham in Wiltshire, and brought here in 1831.

It seems fairly certain that this tower carried no spire until the end of the seventeenth century. Then Henry Winstanley, a local man, designed the curious but rather endearing wooden lantern seen in the engraving of 1784 (124), apparently as a kind of try-out for the first, ill-fated Eddystone lighthouse, which in 1703 cost him his life. By 1831 the whole tower was in a dangerous condition,

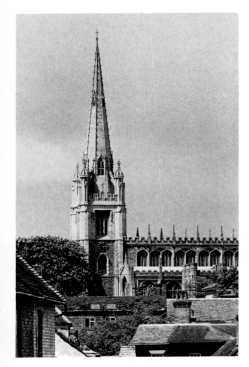

123. The Parish Church of St Mary the Virgin, from the south

124. St Mary's in an engraving of 1784

125. Parish Church, Interior of Nave, looking west

and it was decided to demolish most of it and rebuild, adding an entirely new spire. The architect was Thomas Rickman, who had just completed what is today his most famous work, the New Court at St John's College, Cambridge. He chose Bath stone because, although it entailed a long journey by canal and river, it was at this time one of the least expensive limestones in England. To support its great weight, however, the tower was given a lining of brick. This spire (87) is less original that Winstanley's lantern, but certainly more dignified. At Saffron Walden every other view is pervaded by its commanding presence. It soars to 193 feet.

In this exposed situation, some of this not very tough stone decayed. For the recent restoration (1979–80) they went back to Monk's Park for some more: the absolutely correct thing to do, although not always possible nowadays since, unhappily, so many quarries have closed.

The rest of the church is wholly in the Perpendicular style: the rebuilding was begun about 1470 and finished in 1526. To step inside is to experience at once its great nobility (125). The fine proportions, the slender moulded piers, the very lofty arcades, the tower arch, the wide and spacious aisles: all contribute to a general impression of magnificence. And this is indeed architecturally the finest church in Essex, and the largest.

Moreover, the names of the architects (who were then termed master masons) are known. A building contract of 1485, which came to light fairly recently, reveals that they were Simon Clerk, master mason of the Abbey of Bury St Edmunds for over forty years, acting in partnership (for by then he was an old man) with none other than the great John Wastell (c. 1460–c. 1515), who

126. Parish Church, Interior of Nave, looking east

was later to design such masterpieces as Bell Harry, the central tower of Canterbury Cathedral, the wonderful fan-vault and much else at King's College Chapel, Cambridge, and almost certainly the retro-choir at Peterborough, as well as Great St Mary at Cambridge, St James (now the Cathedral) at Bury St Edmunds, and probably, Dr John Harvey believes, the nave at Lavenham.

The stone for the lower parts of the piers would seem to have been brought from Ketton in Rutland. It would have been floated down the Welland in flat-bottomed boats. If it passed Spalding it would have reached King's Lynn by way of the Wash, and thence would have been brought up the Ouse and so into the Cam, which, as we shall see, flows through the park of Audley End. A much shorter route may, however, have been available. There is a possibility that the boats could have been rowed or poled over meres and through marshes on the fringes of fens which have long since been drained, without having to travel nearly as far north as The Wash. This is an interesting subject on which sufficient documentation to be able to arrive at a firm conclusion is unfortunately lacking.

Other limestones besides Ketton were also used, including, again, clunch. This was employed for the spandrels of the nave arcade (in one of which, facing the south aisle, occurs, as already noted, a representation of the saffron crocus) and of the chancel arch, all of which are elaborately carved (126). It was very easy – all too easy, sometimes – to carve this soft stone; but here the enrichment is perfectly acceptable and even welcome. What is a good deal less welcome is the heavy reddish-brown oak rood screen, inserted as recently as 1924. This was a gift which, had it been offered today, would, I hope, not be accepted. If a screen is needed at all, how much better to have an elegant open one in wrought iron, inspired perhaps by the beautiful screen in the church of All Saints (now the Cathedral) at Derby.

Two other blots are the heavy pews, excessive in number and at variance with the building's cool spaciousness, and the Victorian glass. Fortunately a good many of the big windows still retain clear glass; especially effective is the west window of the north aisle, looking out on to enormous trees. Nor is the Victorian east window to be despised; no information has been forthcoming about either the maker or the date. But in the aisles much of the glass is feebleness itself, with insipid drawing and so much overpainting that very little light filters through. This is to deny the whole artistic purpose of stained glass, which should be jewel-like.

Formerly in the chancel, but removed in 1793 to the south chapel, is the tomb of Lord Audley (127), surrounded by an iron railing. The material is a kind of black slate known as 'touch', imported from Belgium. This was a prestige material for those who could afford it, cherished because its smooth grain made it so good for carving. But only the achievement of arms at the head of the tomb is now well preserved.

The man commemorated did not deserve so handsome a monument. Thomas Audley (128), who died in 1544, was one of Henry VIII's toadies: an obsequious opportunist who was only too willing to step into Sir Thomas More's shoes as Chancellor of England after More had told the King, his erstwhile friend, that he could not countenance either the break with Rome or the royal divorce. Later it was Audley who presided over the Court which passed sentence of death on both More and Fisher, the Bishop of Rochester. Thomas Fuller, the Caroline divine and wit, whose famous book, *Worthies of England*, was not published until after his death in 1661, said of this monument that the stone was not blacker than the soul, nor was it harder than the heart, of the man whose bones lay beneath it. Yet at the Suppression Audley got a big picking. Henry rewarded him with Walden Abbey.

Of the Abbey nothing survives, nor did Audley build a house on the site. He left no son either; but his only surviving daughter married the 4th Duke of Norfolk, and it was their son, Thomas Howard, Lord Treasurer to James I, who built, very close to where the

127. Parish Church, Tomb of Lord Audley

128. Thomas Audley (detail)

monastery had been, Audley End House (129), named after his grandfather. The park stretches right up to the town of Saffron Walden, in whose parish it has always been.

It was once the largest house in England: more than twice its present size. 'Too large for a King, but I suppose it might do for a Lord Treasurer,' James I is believed to have said, on the one and only occasion when he came here. Soon after it was completed, Howard, who had been made Earl of Suffolk, was charged with embezzling public funds and was committed to the Tower. He was tried, found guilty, and fined £30,000, a huge sum in those days. But he was soon released and, although disgraced, was able to retire to Audley End, where in 1626 he died.

In 1669 the mansion was bought by Charles II, who required a palace as a *pied-à-terre* on the way to and from the races at Newmarket. As so often where transactions with the Stuarts were concerned, the purchase money, £50,000, was never fully paid, and in 1701 the fifth Earl of Suffolk got it back for nothing. He could not afford to maintain this vast house, and in 1721, on the advice of Vanbrugh, three sides of the great outer courtyard were demolished. The removal of the east range of the inner court, with the beautiful Long Gallery, followed about 1749. Yet even in its truncated state Audley End is about the same size as Hatfield.

Seen from the main road to the west (130), this house looks rather fine. It is built of limestone – largely, again, of Ketton stone – which in Essex was a colossal piece of extravagance. For Hatfield, which was being built at exactly the same time, Robert Cecil was content to use brick; but not so this grandee. For him it had to be limestone and nothing else. To Evelyn it was 'a cheerful piece of Gothic building, or rather *antico moderno*'. Close to, it has to be said that this is not one of the most beguiling of the great Jacobean houses. Nor is there any longer much about it that is Jacobean: it has undergone so much later alteration. Especially unfortunate is the disappearance of all the leaded lights from the windows, which today are sadly vacant-looking. For this the responsibility may not, for once, rest with the Victorians, for soon after the death in 1745 of the tenth Earl of Suffolk and the last to live here, it is recorded that many of the windows were without glass, and blocked up with sacking.

At this time also the interior was stripped of all its furniture. Almost the only enjoyable survival from Thomas Howard's time, inside the house, is the ceiling of the Saloon. This is divided by strapwork and pendants into compartments, which are enriched with representations of ships, sea-birds, mermaids, whales and fabulous sea-monsters: all great fun! There are, however, other pleasures here and there. The Saloon is approached from the Hall by an elegant double staircase inserted by Vanbrugh, with a beautiful wrought-iron handrail. Another unexpected feature is the Chapel which, apart from the garish window, is Gothick* at its

129. Audley End House, Park and the Town of Saffron Walden from Ring Hill

130. Audley End House, west front

---

* This term is now in general use to indicate the Georgian interpretation of Gothic, which was unscholarly and essentially frivolous but often very entertaining. Horace Walpole was a leading exponent.

129

30

most engaging. Dating from 1786, it has recently been restored with skill and taste.

But it is the Park which offers the greatest pleasures here. This was mainly an eighteenth-century creation, with 'Capability' Brown in fine form. It was his idea to make the great lawn in front of the house, and to dam the River Cam to form a narrow lake. At the same time Robert Adam was commissioned to design the lovely triple-arched Bridge (133) which still carries a public road. That was in 1763, and in the same year he was also responsible for the little Circular Temple on Ring Hill (131) half a mile to the west, the site of the Iron Age fort referred to on page 75. Set against a belt of dark trees it provides a pleasant 'eye-catcher' for the house. Twenty years later he designed another vista feature: the so-called Palladian Bridge over the Cam (134), with a teahouse in the centre. This pretty conceit is now known as the Tea House Bridge.

The latest of the Park's 'ornaments', the Temple of Concord to the east of the house (132), was not by Adam but by R. F. Brettingham. It was erected in 1791 to commemorate, it is said, the recovery of George III from what unhappily turned out to be only his first attack of insanity.

In the late 1830s plans were drawn up for the construction of a railway line from London to Cambridge. There was never much chance of its passing through Saffron Walden; the town was too far to the east, and anyway leading families like the Gibsons did not want it. (Later the town had its own branch-line, long since closed and dismantled.) But the promoters wanted their railway to pass along the east side of Ring Hill, close to the A11 road, and therefore between the house and the Circular Temple. The third Lord Braybrooke, the owner of Audley End at that time, insisted that the line went on the other side of the hill, although this involved two tunnels (one of which, on its south side, bears the Braybrooke coat of arms). Thereby, in the preservation of the landscape, he did a service not only to himself and his family but to posterity too. It has,

131. Circular Temple on Ring Hill, Audley End Park

132. Temple of Concord, Audley End Park

133. The Bridge, Audley End Park

134. Tea House Bridge, Audley End Park

132

133

134

135. Lion House

however, meant that the people of Saffron Walden have rather further to go now to reach their station, Audley End, than would otherwise have been the case. Incidentally, this station, although marred by the later addition of a *porte-cochère* and by a recent building adjoining, is in essence a classical design of distinct charm.

Just outside the Park wall, and close to Adam's Bridge, is a beautifully proportioned little brick house, with low-pitched slate roofs and Gothick windows, which belongs to the early years of the nineteenth century (135). It does not look at all like its name, which is Lion House: but this it owes to being just opposite Lion Gate, erected in 1786 as the Park's main entrance. (The Lion is of Coade stone, of which there will be more to say at Lewes.)

Nearby is the entrance to the former estate village of Audley End, which consists of hardly more than a single street. With one exception, a small house half-way along built of flint, all the cottages are timber-framed, but as they have all been plastered over and whitened, this is not immediately apparent. Much of the plaster shows incised pargeting. As often with cottages, the Georgian-style windows slide sideways to open.

At the far end of the street are a farm and St Mark's College (136), built about 1600 as an almshouse, and now a home for retired clergy: a secluded place, ranged around two very plain courtyards. This, although a good deal restored, has old brickwork and good hand-made tiles.

So all the local materials are present in this hamlet. In this

136. St Mark's College

137. 1 Freshwell Street

respect, the tiny village of Audley End is an echo of Saffron Walden in miniature: an excellent exemplar of the pattern of English building. Yet in another respect they could hardly be more different. Audley End's single street is a quiet cul-de-sac.

Saffron Walden, on the other hand, is a martyr to traffic. In Bridge Street, through which the A130 road from Cambridge to Chelmsford enters the town, many properties have received direct hits, usually from lorries or motor bicycles. During the last few years the Eight Bells Inn (138), a timber-framed Elizabethan building with a charming modern wrought-iron sign brought here from Watford, has been hit no fewer than six times.

What can be done? Neither an outer by-pass nor an inner relief road are financially viable here. The only hope would seem to be to signpost through traffic by routes that avoid Saffron Walden altogether, on to the M11, which was built to carry it, but on to which at present there is, regrettably, no access road within several miles of the town.

It is the jettied buildings, those with overhanging upper storeys, that are specially vulnerable, particularly where streets are narrow. Outside the former Sun Inn, with its precious pargeting, the pavement has been extended, and luckily Church Street is not one of the major through roads. But Bridge Street is, and sensitively designed, unobtrusive bollards to protect specially vulnerable buildings, like the one outside the cottage at the corner of Freshwell Street (137), would appear to be the only practical solution. There should be a lot more of them, and the stronger they are the better.

Within a few months of the passing of the Civic Amenities Act in 1967, Essex County Council declared the whole place a Conservation Area. In 1974 this was granted 'outstanding' status, and two years later, very soon after the Historic Buildings Council for England started work, a Town Scheme was set up. All these measures assisted the giving of grants for renovation, and in recent years much excellent work has been accomplished. Long may it continue, for Saffron Walden is a compact and singularly unspoiled country town.

138. The Eight Bells, Bridge Street

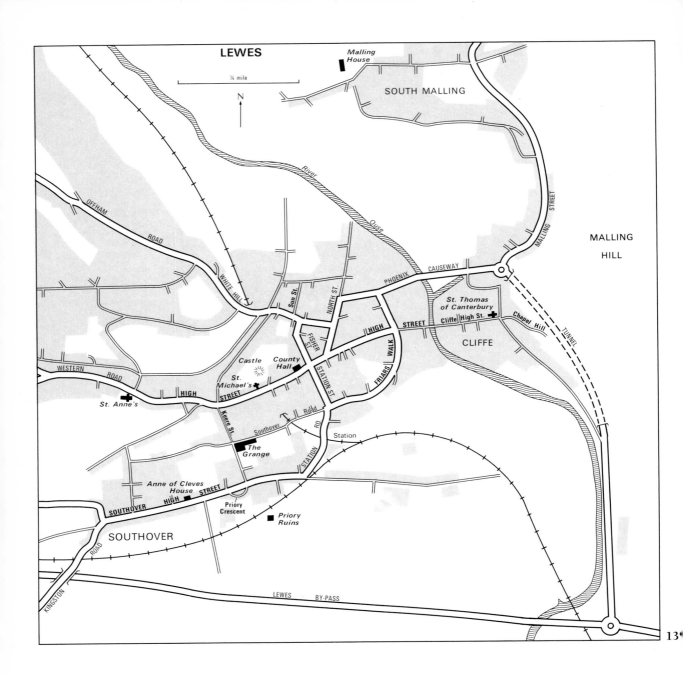

LEWES

¼ mile

N

Malling House

SOUTH MALLING

MALLING HILL

OFFHAM ROAD

River

Ouse

WHITE HILL

MALLING STREET

PHOENIX CAUSEWAY

Sun St.

NORTH ST.

St. Thomas of Canterbury

Chapel Hill

TUNNEL

FISHER ST.

HIGH STREET

Cliffe High St.

CLIFFE

WESTERN ROAD

Castle

County Hall

WALK

St. Michael's

HIGH STREET

STATION ST.

FRIARS

St. Anne's

Keere St.

Southover

RD.

Station

Road

The Grange

STATION

Anne of Cleves House

SOUTHOVER HIGH STREET

Priory Crescent

Priory Ruins

SOUTHOVER

ROAD

KINGSTON ROAD

LEWES   BY-PASS

13

4. Lewes

Lewes. Rather an odd name, is it not, when you come to think about it? The correct pronunciation is loo-ez, not loo-ess, and certainly not l'yew-ez (to rhyme with 'new'). But how could a foreigner, including a foreign Englishman, be sure? Philologists used to say that the name derived from the Old English word *laes* (dative, *laeswe*), meaning pasture; but the English Place Name Society is now confident that the source of the name is '*hlaew*', which in Old English means a hill.

And certainly, looking at Lewes, we think of hills rather than pastures. Nothing about this place is more memorable than its site. The town is built along a spur of land which drops away abruptly on every side but the west. This spur is situated, as a plaque near the upper end of the High Street records, exactly on the Greenwich meridian.

No natural feature of southern England is more deservedly loved than the South Downs, a marvellous swathe of chalk hills which runs, slightly south of due east, the whole length of Sussex until it plunges into the sea at Beachy Head, just above Eastbourne. This is frequently thought of as one continuous range, but that is an over-simplification. For one thing, in their long journey across Sussex the South Downs are pierced by four rivers: the Arun, which reaches the sea at Littlehampton; the Adur, at Shoreham; the Cuckmere, east of Seaford; and, between these two last, the most important of the four, the Sussex Ouse, which emerges at Newhaven but first meets the Downs at Lewes. At this point the Downs have become distinctly fragmented. The long narrow hill dropping steeply to the river, along which the town itself grew up (139), and still more obviously the abruptly faced Malling Hill opposite, on the left bank of the Ouse, can be regarded as outliers from the main range. Perhaps that is why this site seems to have been of no interest to the Romans: nor indeed for almost half a millennium after their departure. Documentation related to the Saxon period is very scarce, but it is known that coins were minted here under King Athelstan (925–940). It seems probable, therefore, that the town originated some time during the eighth century: perhaps not much before 900.

A few years ago, at a small gathering of friends, someone posed the question, 'If you did not live in London, where would you best like to be?' I waited, listening to others pitching their tents in Herefordshire, the Cotswolds, Dorset, Devon, even Suffolk. When my turn came, I answered without hestitation (for I had already given the matter much thought). 'I know exactly where I would choose. It would be on a south-facing slope two miles north of the South Downs, looking at them.' I will not dwell here on the other advantages: one of England's warmest counties, and her sunniest, and the excellent train service to the metropolis. I am thinking now of the visual delights.

The gently billowing outline of the Downs suggests their

140. View from the Castle keep, looking east towards Malling Hill

structure: chalk, soft enough to have been shaped by aeons of wind and rain (140). There are no crags here, no rocky outcrops. Chalk, cut into blocks, could be used as a building stone at certain places where nothing else was available, but not at Lewes. There is, however, one hard substance present in the upper layers of the chalk formation: flint. So in medieval times, if you were anywhere near the South Downs and you wanted to build with something stronger and more durable than wood, you either had to import stone from afar, which was expensive, or use flint. The Norman invaders lost no time in appreciating the value of Lewes's hilly spur as a natural strongpoint for a castle; it was, and still is, built of flint. And that intractable stone continued to be one of the town's more important building materials until little more than a hundred years ago, and is still used in modern buildings as a constituent of concrete aggregate.

The builder of the original Castle was not the Conqueror himself but one of his closest and most privileged companions, William de Warenne, who on the accession of William Rufus was to become the Earl of Surrey (he was granted lands in Surrey and Norfolk as well as Sussex). Not a great deal survives, but Lewes Castle had one most unusual feature: instead of one *motte* (or mound), there were two. No one has ever been able to explain why. The purpose of the *motte* in a Norman Castle was to elevate the keep, the place of refuge in times of danger, to a position of still greater strength. At Lewes both mounds were supposedly crowned at one time by roughly circular shell-keeps. But Brack Mount, 200 yards to the north-east, the lower of the two and the first to be constructed — it has been suggested that there may have been a change of plan — carries no buildings now.

Both these huge mounds were man-made; the chalk Downs do not produce natural shapes like these. The mounds, however, are also chalk: lumps of chalk, shaped roughly into blocks and laboriously hauled up. Under the present covering of earth and grass, that is what they still are; and in the back wall of the garage of Brack Mound House, which was once the coach house, they are exposed.

The surviving keep (142) is on the south-western motte, which is the higher. It has undergone a good deal of restoration, and the two projecting towers, which much improve the skyline, were a thirteenth-century addition. The stone, wherever one looks, is almost all flint, and most of it is set in rough layers or coursed. Here and there this coursing, as at Richmond in Yorkshire, is of the herring-bone type, which is always indicative of early Norman construction.

After the death of the last de Warenne in 1347, the Castle stood empty and, with the assistance of some of the local citizens, who broke in and vandalised it, quickly fell into decay. (Human nature does not change, alas.) The new owner, the Earl of Arundel, was not interested. Eventually, in 1620, what remained of the domestic buildings was demolished for the sake of the materials. In the eighteenth century the keep was leased to the owner of Barbican House, just below, who treated it as a kind of super-gazebo, although until a new spiral staircase was put into the southern tower early in the last century is was not possible to climb to the top. The view from the top storey remains the principal attraction (140).

The entry into the bailey, the area of the Castle within the curtain wall, was through an early Norman gatehouse (of which part can be seen on the left of the view from the keep). This also

141. Castle, the Barbican

142. Castle, the Keep

143. Section of the Town Walls

displays large flints laid with rough herring-bone coursing. Apart from the wall there is nothing to be seen here of the Castle but some vaulted cellars under what was once the Great Hall. Part of the bailey is a bowling green, and has been so at least since the eighteenth and perhaps even from the seventeenth century. But in front of the Norman gatehouse was erected, early in the fourteenth century and only about a generation before the Castle was abandoned, what is now much the most impressive surviving part of the whole complex: the Barbican (141). Of this kind of outer gatehouse, it is one of the biggest and best examples in England.

It was built in the Castle Ditch, a broad dry moat, which had to be crossed by a drawbridge. Now the road runs on an embankment. The contrast between the flintwork on the face of the embanked road and that on the outer face of the Barbican itself, above the entrance, is striking. On the latter the flints have been carefully knapped — that is to say, split open to display their glassy insides — and laid in fairly regular courses: a decidedly early example of this technique. For the dressings — the archway itself, the quoins, the corbelled-out bases of the bartizans or projecting turrets (of which only the left-hand one survives intact), the cross-shaped arrowloops and, above all, the bold machicolations (the projecting parapets with holes in the floor through which could be dropped missiles or whatever) — they even brought in some green sandstone from the Weald. Some of this stone has had to be renewed. It has not lasted nearly as well as the virtually indestructible flints.

Spanning the centuries, flintwork turns up in many different guises at Lewes. There is Keere (pronounced 'care') Street, for example (144), with a precipitous hill down which George IV, when Prince of Wales, is said to have driven a coach for a wager. (He was always short of cash!) In addition to some of the houses, cobblestones, mainly of flint, were used for the paved water-course which runs down the centre. The local people call them 'petrified kidneys', so oddly shaped are some of them. As they look water-rolled, it seems probable that they came from a nearby beach. The most likely one is Newhaven, easily accessible after the opening of the Lower Ouse Navigation at the end of the eighteenth century. An Act of 1806 provided for the cleaning and paving of the streets, and it was probably then that these very effective cobblestones were laid.

At the bottom of the hill there is a good external view of the Town Walls which, although now coursed with brick at wide intervals, are also predominantly flint (143). Only two stretches on the west side of the town, and at the south-west corner, are now visible. They go back to 1269, and here, as at the Castle keep, the flints are purely functional without any refinements at all.

Still less attractive flintwork can be seen at the sad remains of St Pancras Priory. This was also founded by William de Warenne, with his wife Gundrada. It was the first Cluniac monastery in England, and the plan of the church, with double transepts and an array of apsidal chapels, resembled that of Cluny itself. Although

144. Keere Street

145. 140 High Street

never as rich as Battle Abbey, this monastic church was bigger than its diocesan church, Chichester Cathedral. At the Dissolution the Priory had the misfortune to be granted to Thomas Cromwell himself, the arch-destroyer. The little that survived of the east end of the church, the chapter house and the east and south walls of the cloister, was finally swept away by the railway line from Lewes to Brighton, which cuts right across the site. Fragments of some of the monastic buildings still remain, mostly very amorphous, for, as I observed at Saffron Walden, flint, of all building materials, yields the most unpicturesque ruins.

But the walls of houses built or faced with flints are often well worth examining. In the High Street, a range of three adjoining houses on the north side, Nos 139, 140 and 141, provide an object lesson in flint construction. Nearly all these flints are knapped, except the top storey of No. 140 (145) which was obviously a later addition, and done very crudely indeed, perhaps because at this time it had already been decided to mask the front of this house behind a coat of stucco. A few years ago this mask was removed, and in this case rightly so, for although the top storey is unworthy the rest is excellent, with carefully coursed flints, many of them almost egg-shaped, and beautifully pointed brick surrounds to all

146. 141 High Street

the windows, not to mention the delightful doorway with its elliptically-arched fanlight. What a pity that the ground-floor windows have been deprived of their glazing bars.

No. 141 (146) also suffers in this respect, and at the time of writing is in need of redecoration; but if sympathetically restored (the dormers also badly need attention), this could be the finest house of the three. Many of the flints were not only knapped but squared, a choice refinement permitting of a great reduction in the amount of mortar used, which is always the bugbear of flint, both visually and from the practical standpoint, since mortar, unlike flint, is by no means indestructible. In addition, this house has its flints set off by elegant Portland limestone, employed for the quoins, the cornice, the architraves of all the windows, the Doric porch, and the plinth for the railing.

At No. 139 (147) (which, despite the date on the rainwater head, would not appear to have any connection with 1654) the window surrounds and the modillioned cornice are of wood. The upper windows are not as well proportioned as in the two adjoining houses, but the presence of all the glazing bars is a great asset. What is not so good is the flintwork, much of which is uncoursed and anything but urbane. There has also been some bad

147

148

repointing, with the wrong coloured mortar (and too much of it) behind the downpipe and between the two windows to the left of it, and also on the stone-slated roof. (The blocked arch on the right indicates that there was once a driveway here, presumably through to the stables.)

Because the shapes are so eccentric, flint benefits tremendously from regular coursing; and if the flints can be all about the same size, that is better still. For a modest early nineteenth-century house front in Sun Street (148) they must have gone to the beach at Newhaven or Seaford and picked out a whole lot of flint cobbles of roughly the same size, all changed into large eggs by the action of the sea. This made coursing very much easier. For the dressings here they used brick which has been painted black: an excellent foil to the white cobbles. They gave themselves a lot of trouble, in fact, but it was well worth it.

When building with flint, some other material always has to be introduced for the angles, whether of a wall, a door of a window. It was the impossibility of achieving clean angles in flint that prompted the erection of so many round church towers in the flint areas. But that was chiefly in East Anglia. Lewes has one example, unhappily maltreated. The little round tower of St Michael's church (149), one of the only three in Sussex, is said to date from the thirteenth century, although it looks earlier. When water started penetrating the mortar it was given a coating of pebble-dash: so much cheaper than re-mortaring!*

In contrast, the knapped flintwork on the south wall of the church, abutting on to the High Street, is among the best the town has to show. It dates from 1748 and is much enhanced by the use of Portland stone for the dressings. What a contrast this makes with the aggressively coarse flintwork, with harsh red brick dressings, of the adjacent belfry of 1882 attached to The Church House. This is flint building at its most disagreeable.

In general it must be said that red brick is not a pleasing foil for flint, except when employed discreetly and in very small quantities. If stone is too expensive, dressings of 'white' brick look much better than red, as can be seen at St Michael's Court, half-way down Keere Street, which was built in 1846 as an almshouse. But red brick was used again in combination with flint four years later, for what is in many respects a very handsome building: the Prison, on the hill at the far western end of the town. Flint, we observe, was still being employed on a large scale here as late as 1850.

Apart from flint, which was the principal material of all the fourteen parish churches (now reduced to six, of which one is redundant), stone in the buildings of Lewes is rather scarce. When masonry was required here in the Middle Ages, it was either of Caen oolite imported from Normandy, of Quarr limestone brought from the Isle of Wight, or of Wealden sandstone, as at the Barbican. The archway

149. St Michael's Church, High Street

*The effective sculpture of the Archangel Michael, attached to the wall of the tower, dates from 1976. It was presumably inspired by Epstein's at Coventry Cathedral. The sculptor is Harry Phillips and the material fibreglass.

147. 139 High Street

148. 19 Sun Street

150. Southover Grange

of the Castle's Norman gatehouse is Caen, and it was used at St Pancras Priory, as at Chichester Cathedral, for the piers and arches, dressings and carved details of the church, and for certain outbuildings, notably the Infirmary Chapel and the Prior's Lodging. Much of this limestone was either pillaged or sold. The Lodging was the only portion retained intact by Thomas Cromwell, who wanted it as a house for his son. As such it did not serve for long, for in 1568 it was accidentally burnt.

After this fire many blocks of Caen stone, at Lewes too valuable to waste, were transported a few hundred yards to build Southover Grange (150), the one stone house here that is earlier than the eighteenth century. The builder was William Newton, steward to the lord of the manor, who at this time was the Earl of Dorset. Late in life he married John Evelyn's grandmother, then a widow, which is how the future diarist came to live in this house from 1630 to 1637. He went to the local Grammar School. His father wanted him to go to Eton, but he refused, 'being terrified with the report of the severe discipline there'. 'This perverseness of mine', he was to write later, 'I have since a thousand times deplored.' This charming (although much altered) Elizabethan house now belongs to the town; a great asset is the large garden, with some choice trees and the Winterbourne, a fast-flowing, pellucid stream making for the Ouse.

Caen stone can be seen again on the front of a large building, 220–221 (151), at the foot of the High Street, close to the river. This would seem to have always been a pair of mid-eighteenth-century houses, although designed as a single composition. (The bows came later, and later still the maltreatment of the central windows, which could so easily be restored to what they should be.) The Caen stone facing may have been taken from St Pancras Priory or perhaps from one of the eight demolished churches. It is attractive, but unfortunately not very hard: hence the patching below and the cement rendering over the whole of the upper part, which is very disfiguring.

Part of the roof of Southover Grange is also stone, and no doubt it all was originally. These great slabs of Wealden sandstone are known generally as 'Horsham' slates, although, like Aylesbury ducks and Norfolk turkeys, they came from many other places too. Happily a good many survive, scattered about the town (159, 170, 174), for they wear a tremendous air of authority: but sometimes, as at Southover Grange, it will be found that they only cover part of a roof. This is because their immense weight (a single slab at the eaves can weigh over 60 lbs) caused the supporting timbers to sag, or even to cave in completely, and in renewing the roof some lighter material – often, like tiles or Welsh slate, not at all appropriate – has been partly substituted.

A specially good example of sandstone roofing-slates can be seen at the church of St Thomas of Canterbury at Cliffe (153). (And Cliffe, across the Ouse from Lewes itself, like South Malling a mile beyond, and Southover across the Winterbourne, is an outlier of the Norman town, now incorporated within its bounds.) The slates at this church can be well seen, for they were laid at an unusually steep pitch. The nave of St Anne's church (to which I shall return) is also roofed with these sandstone slates. The manner in which, on all these roofs, they are carefully graded, from as much, sometimes, as two feet at the base to no more than a few inches at the ridge, is an unfailing source of pleasure.

151. 220–221 High Street

153. St Thomas of Canterbury, Cliffe

152. County Hall, 'Justice'

In the eighteenth century, when Lewes was at the peak of its prosperity, a little stone did come here from farther afield — always, of course, by sea. Newcastle House (154) once belonged to its eponymous Duke, the Whig statesman and head of the Pelham family; his principal house, now gone, was at Halland, a few miles to the north-east, but he also maintained a town house in Lewes. The sundial in the pediment carries the date 1717, but this house was originally built in the 1680s. It was faced with Caen stone: not reused Caen here, but new stone, brought specially from Normandy. Unhappily it decayed, and what we see today is a near-copy erected in 1929 (and very carefully done) by Sir Reginald Blomfield. To face it he used not Caen stone but Portland.

Portland stone in any quantity did not appear in Lewes until 1812, when it was employed to face the new County Hall next door to Newcastle House (155). This is a building with a very distinct personality of its own. The architect was John Johnson of Leicester: it was his very last work, completed when he was eighty. It is a pity that the two end-bays of what was originally a five-bay Tuscan Doric loggia were later filled in. It is now no longer the County Hall but the Crown Courts building. Both this and Newcastle House are law courts.

That this building has, however, always had legal associations is evident from the subjects of the three high-relief panels on the second floor: Mercy, Wisdom and Justice (the one illustrated: 152). These three panels, skilfully executed in a neo-Greek style, and to some eyes, no doubt, rather boring, are in Coade stone, which is not stone at all but a kind of terracotta. It was made by mixing certain clays and sands according to a formula which always remained a closely guarded secret, a confidence which was never broken, and is now lost. Yet from the 1770s, when this product was first launched at Lambeth, Coade's artificial stone, as it was called, enjoyed over half a centry of unrivalled success. Within a few years there was hardly an architect or speculative builder who was not making use of it for sculptural and other ornamental details, generally in the classical style. It has proved astonishingly

154. Newcastle House, High Street

155. County Hall

154

155

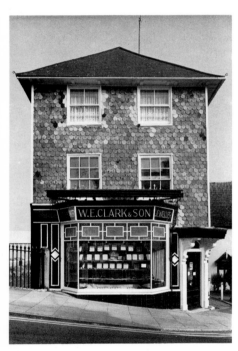

156. 1 Cliffe High Street

durable: far more so, in fact, than have most varieties of stone.

An unexpected material to find here in Sussex is slate: but Lewes — or, to be more exact, Cliffe — can show several examples of slate-hung walls, of which 8–9 Chapel Hill (157) is one. These hung slates were brought, I believe, from Devon or Cornwall in the early years of the nineteenth century. The trade in slates, mainly used for roofs, from the far south-west to south-eastern counties and beyond has a very long history indeed. By as early as 1187, nearly a million Devon slates had been transported for the King's buildings to Winchester alone. Cliffe High Street can show two other houses with hung slates: and it seems to me not without significance that all these three examples are within 200 yards of the river.

On the front of the house adjoining the bridge (156), the pretty slates in the shape of scallops may also have come from the South-West. But if you think that the side of this building has hung slates too you have been taken in, as the builder fully intended that you should be. They are replacements, no more than ten years old, in asbestos. It has to be granted that they succeed surprisingly well.

In the Middle Ages, what was not flint in Lewes was timber-framed. Sussex abounded in wood, and in oak in particular, and every house here, as in so many other medieval towns, had its timber frame. Moreover many still have, although it is usually masked by a later front of brick or plaster. In a few cases the wood frame is still obvious: a good example, dating from the fifteenth century, is the bookshop at the corner of the High Street and Keere Street (158). To illustrate how, in a structure of this kind, the subsidiary timbers can be chopped about almost at will, there are the opening above the right-hand door, cut not so long ago to receive an old milestone from a building opposite, now demolished, and, on the jettied floor above, the side window with the view along the street.

In Southover High Street is the building known as Anne of Cleves House (159), which is now a museum of crafts and local history. Although there is no evidence that she ever came here, this

158. 99–100 High Street

159. Anne of Cleves House, Southover High Street

158

159

160. St Anne's Church

was one of the properties made over by Henry VIII to 'the great Flanders mare' as the price of ridding himself of her. It is a veritable compendium of almost all the local materials. There are flints, enormous sandstone roofing slates, roof tiles, hung tiles and brick: but basically, although very much restored and altered, this is a timber-framed building. The porch with oversailing gable is dated 1599, and the gabled wing in the foreground is also the outcome of later alteration. But the core of the house is a century earlier and belongs to what is known as the Wealden type. The special characteristic of the Wealden house is that, whereas the central hall is recessed between two jettied ends, the hipped roof runs continuously from one end of the house to the other; it did this here until the west wing was altered. Thus the projection of the eaves above the big hall window is considerable and requires additional support, which is provided by a pair of curved braces springing from the jettied wings in a direction parallel to the front.* The overhang of the eaves is here masked by a curved plaster cove, with timbers shaped accordingly: a pleasing feature which is chiefly to be seen in the timber-framed buildings of Cheshire and Lancashire, and is not common in the south-east.

When tiles are of wood they are known as shingles. They are always renewals — they must be, because they never last more than a century, and usually less. They are a rare sight in England now except on church spires, but the south-eastern counties still have plenty of these: Lewes has two. Shingles surmount the round tower of St Michael's church (149). They can also be seen at what is probably the best of what I am bound to say is not a very distinguished brood of churches: St Anne. This has a stocky flint tower (160) capped by a short shingled spire of what is called the splay-footed type (which should not be confused with the broach spire, although it constantly is). What a pity that this attractive composition should have been marred by an ill-placed chimney.

Oak shingles are now unobtainable, and these are almost certainly of machine-sawn Canadian cedarwood. Although they cannot equal the beauty of English oak, they are a very good second-best, for they soon weather to a pleasant grey. They are also easier to handle than oak, having a close, straight grain, less prone to warp. As they can also be produced in larger sizes and at a substantially lower cost, the English wood is unable to compete.

Lewes in medieval times was not particularly prosperous. It has never at any time had very much industry although, surprisingly perhaps, it used to be quite a busy port. But from the last quarter of the seventeenth century it began to flourish as an administrative and social centre. It was, after all, the county town of Sussex. Some people built new houses. But a good many, at a time when timber framing had come to be regarded as almost unbearably old-fashioned, had to be content with fitting up their framed houses with smart new fronts. Here, it would seem, lay the origin of Lewes's most original building material, the brick-tile.

*These can also be seen at 41–43 Castle Street, Saffron Walden (109).

Brick tiles, or 'mathematical' tiles as they are usually called, although, so far as I am aware, nobody has ever been able to explain why, occurred at various places in the southern and eastern counties, from Wiltshire to Norfolk, but especially in Sussex and Kent. They are by no means peculiar to Lewes, nor did they make their first appearance here; but, with the probable exception of Brighton, there is no other English town which has so many. Lewes has more than sixty buildings in all, partly or wholly faced with them, in a great variety of styles and combinations.*

The large majority of people have certainly never seen a mathematical tile, or M-tile, as I usually call it. Or rather, they have not seen one *knowingly*. For it was never intended that these tiles should be recognised for what they are. The dimensions vary considerably, but the profile of the usual M-tile is as in plate 162. Only the lower, vertical face is exposed. The rest is masked by the next course above.

How were they attached to the wall? With timber-framed buildings — and the very large majority of houses upon which M-tiles were used were of this kind — there were two ways. Where the infilling of the framed building was wattle-and-daub or lath-and-

*On the subject of mathematical tiles I should like gratefully to acknowledge the assistance which I have received from two people who have made a special study of this subject: Mr Edward O'Shea, of Lewes (who has also read and kindly commented on the whole chapter), and Mr Maurice Exwood, of Ewell, Surrey, another place where they can be seen. Papers by Mr Terence Paul Smith and Mr David Duckham have also been read with profit.

161. Bartholomew House: detail

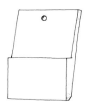

162. A mathematical tile

163. 213 High Street

164. 27–29 Sun Street

plaster, the usual practice was to cover the entire wall with soft-wood boarding, on to which the tiles were then not only nailed but bedded in lime putty. Where the infilling was brick — nogging, as it is called — the boards could be omitted and the tiles bedded directly on to the old fabric, again with plenty of lime putty, and nails as well wherever it was possible to knock them in. Striking evidence for the important role of the putty was revealed in 1979 when, to facilitate the northern approach to the new road tunnel under Malling Hill, two cottages in Malling Street had to be demolished. Both were faced with black-glazed M-tiles, with red unglazed dressings. It was discovered that most of the iron nails had rusted away, yet, although alongside a busy main road with incessant traffic vibration, not one of these tiles had slipped.

It used to be thought (and by me, among others) that the main reason for making these tiles, which were never very cheap, was to avoid the Brick Tax, which was first imposed in 1784. It has now been established that tiles were not only liable to the tax from the outset, but initially at a higher rate than for brick, and furthermore, that a considerable proportion of the brick-tiles at Lewes ante-date the tax — some, in fact, go back to the 1740s. In the second half of the eighteenth century, they were *the* Lewes speciality. The primary reason for them was, quite simply, fashion. 'Correct' taste in the Georgian age required that timber-framing should be masked. Cladding with M-tiles was also marginally cheaper than with bricks and carried the further advantage of encroaching hardly at all upon the pavement of the street.

The black M-tiles appeared rather later than the red. It was believed that their glazed surface afforded protection against a salt-laden atmosphere: hence their popularity in Brighton. At Lewes two modest early nineteenth-century examples in Sun Street (164) are typical. The glaze was obtained by coating each tile with a lead-based powder before firing. The glazed M-tiles were always laid, as here, with a bond consisting entirely of headers, which produces a finely meshed surface effect. To achieve this, every alternate course has to start with a half-tile known as a 'closer'.

The better the tiles, of course, the more difficult they are to identify: they were intended to look just like bricks, and at best they do. At 213 High Street (163), a handsome house whose ground floor windows have undergone a distressing and unaccountable mutilation which I hope will very soon be remedied, even the Department of the Environment's investigator was taken in. This building is in fact a good deal earlier than it appears to be from the front, and is faced not, as stated in the Department's list, with painted bricks but with M-tiles, all, again, laid with header bond.

Often, nevertheless, M-tiles are not difficult to detect. Bartholomew House (165), just below the Castle, another early nineteenth-century building which is faced with black-glazed M-tiles, exhibits a whole quiver of clues. The first point to be noticed is the odd arrangement of the windows. Openings in this sort of relationship, with the corners nearly touching, would never be designed like this if the material were brick. This must be a framed structure: and before the age of ferro-concrete, that meant timber-framed. Nor do

165. Bartholomew House

the window-heads have anything suggestive of arches: another tell-tale.

But most revealing of all is the treatment of the angles. Corners were always a problem with M-tiles. Specially moulded angle-tiles were the best solution, but they were expensive, and it is doubtful whether there are any in Lewes. Most people had to make do with slender wooden boards fixed vertically, and at the time of writing there is a section missing at Bartholomew House, which reveals how the tiles were fixed, with plenty of lime putty to hold them firm (161). The plain wooden board is also easy to see at 8–9 Chapel Hill, Cliffe (157), where upstairs, the east face is slate-hung whereas the south face has M-tiles.

The setting of the window-frames flush with the wall is another pointer, evident in all these examples. At Bartholomew House the window apertures are lined with thin wooden boards exactly like those used at the corners. At 27 – 29 Sun Street a slender board over the pediment of the (alas) harlequin-painted door-case marks the front edge of the party-wall between these two little houses (164).

166. 199–200 High Street

In better-class houses faced with M-tiles, such as numbers 199–200 High Street (166), the thin wooden strips at the corners would give place to rusticated quoins; but these would also be of wood, painted to give a 'stone' effect. They certainly look much better than the boards.

Other tell-tales become evident whenever things go wrong. When buildings faced with M-tiles develop bulges, or when a few of the tiles start to slip, detection becomes easy. Examples of both these can be found at Lewes; and in either circumstance repairs are unfortunately very difficult. Replacement of a missing tile with cement, tinted to the colour of the rest but scarcely ever achieving a good match, is invariably disagreeable.

The imposition of excise duties on bricks and tiles would seem neither to have increased nor decreased the initial popularity of M-tiles at Lewes or elsewhere. The taxes, first levied in 1784, were raised for both in 1794. But after that, whereas there were two more increases for bricks, on M-tiles the duty remained un-changed. So after 1797 tiles enjoyed a tax advantage. Moreover, the duties on tiles were repealed in 1833; on bricks not until 1850.

All the earlier buildings faced with M-tiles were originally timber-framed, but some of the later ones were designed from the outset to be faced with them. A good example is the Friends' Meeting House (167), erected in 1784: a charming little pale pink building, with black-glazed M-tiles, produced specially (what is called 'purpose-made') to surround the windows. The Jireh Chapel, which harboured a much odder sect, dates from 1805. This too was designed *ab initio* to be faced with M-tiles. It has lovely sand-faced headers on two of its four elevations, and has lately been very sympathetically restored.

A generation later, red was quite out of fashion, and for a short time white M-tiles were produced: at least, they were called white, but, as with wines, the word is an elegant euphemism. They can be seen on a house in Southover High Street. Why is it, I wonder, that

168. Brack Mound House

white is considered to be so much more classy than yellow? Sometimes they are described, also inaccurately, as cream. The trade term is 'gaults', for the very good reason that it was from the Gault that this clay was obtained (cf. p. 88).

The houses of Lewes reveal a marked predilection for bow-windows, and I believe that this may be not unconnected with the popularity here of M-tiles. For bows, the backing boards were usually fixed not horizontally but vertically, on a shallow curve, of which Westgate House, High Street, provides a good example. Structurally, the thinness of the tiles has an obvious advantage over brick. The bows here are carried right up to the eaves, as also at 199 and 200 High Street (166), Georgian semi-detached houses in the grand manner! This is another example (and not the only one) of a building faced with M-tiles which foxed the Department's investigator. These good red tiles are all stretchers, which is unusual. The later dormer is regrettable, and so is the Victorian-isation of all the windows, even though the bows do retain their curved panes, which yield excellent reflections. Not all the bow windows of Lewes are old. They had another period of popularity during the period between the wars. But these are structurally original, and M-tiles certainly provide an ideal facing material.

Bow-windows (as distinct from canted bays) greatly enhance a room internally, but externally they can give much pleasure too. It seems probable that the vogue for them here in the late-Georgian period also carried social, even snobbish, implications. For when a local tradesman was doing so well that his wife no longer had to soil her hands by working, the bow window was just the place where she could sit at leisure and watch the busy world go by.

After about 1850 brick-tiles became less common, in Lewes as elsewhere; fashion was changing again, and anyone who owned a timber-framed house, so far from seeking to mask it, was now more likely to want to display its oaken beams as prominently as possible. Nevertheless, small quantities of these tiles continued to be made nearby, at Burgess Hill, until the 1960s, and they can even now be obtained from one brickyard at Southend in Essex.

Of the normal tile-hanging which is such an adornment to houses all over south-eastern England Lewes also has many good examples, mostly, again, over timber-framing. Hung tiles were considered less urbane in the Georgian period than M-tiles or bricks, but sometimes, as at Brack Mound House (168), both can be seen, juxtaposed. The obvious difference is that hung tiles overlap, and cast attractive shadows. Every tile is also slightly curved: not flat.

Originally they were always suspended from battens or laths with the aid of wooden pegs. Later they might be nailed on. Near the head of each tile a pair of holes was pierced for this purpose. Then, towards the end of the nineteenth century, it became the general practice to provide the tiles with little clay hooks called nibs. These were a great help, on roofs as well as walls; but in high class work every fifth — and in exposed places even every third — course would still be nailed. Wooden boards are again much in evidence at the angles (168). The battens were usually of cleft oak,

169. 163–164 High Street

170. 55 Southover High Street

but poplar and willow were also used quite often. Being very pliable, they could be carried round bow windows without any difficulty. For this the thinness of the tiles was an obvious advantage over bricks.

Sometimes the joints between the tiles are now seen to be filled with mortar; but this is aesthetically a mistake and is due to later 'bodging'. In all the best examples – and 163 and 164 High Street (169) have another good display – the joints are left open, to yield little vertical shadows in addition to the stronger horizontal shadows cast by the overhangs: a delightfully subtle effect.

Characteristic of some of the best examples are those minute variations of tint and of density which help to breathe vitality into a tile-hung wall. The gorgeous terracottas of these beautiful tiles seem to pervade the very air of the town. The tiled roofs, of which Lewes has a great number, are in themselves an enviable possession, but on the walls the reds are still richer; because they hang vertically, rainwater runs off them at once and they do not attract moss nor lichen, as roofs sometimes do. But whether on walls or roofs they must be hand-made to be wholly satisfying: that of course is why good tiles are now so expensive. Machine-made tiles look painfully mechanical, and give no pleasure at all.

In the Victorian period there was great enthusiasm for pattern-making with hung tiles. Various designs were produced: the fish-tail, the beaver-tail, the hammer-head, the scallop, and others.

More than one can be seen on the front of a small villa in Southover High Street (170). The effect is undeniably very busy, but when it was built I have little doubt that it was much admired. The contrast, though, with the massive slabs of Wealden sandstone that cover the roof is truly extraordinary. Today most people probably prefer to dispense with this ornamentation, of which another example, a relentlessly machine-made creation, can be seen on plate 181.

For plain tile-hanging and for roofs the same tiles were used (and still are), the only difference being that on roofs there is a slightly greater overlap. The standard length of a plain tile is $10\frac{1}{2}$ inches. On walls $4\frac{1}{2}$ inches are exposed; on roofs only 4 inches.

Lewes may be described as a place which has had a prolonged love affair with brick: and, given the splendid brick-making properties of the local clays, it is not difficult to understand why. A high proportion of them are sand-faced and hand-moulded, with those

171. 211 High Street

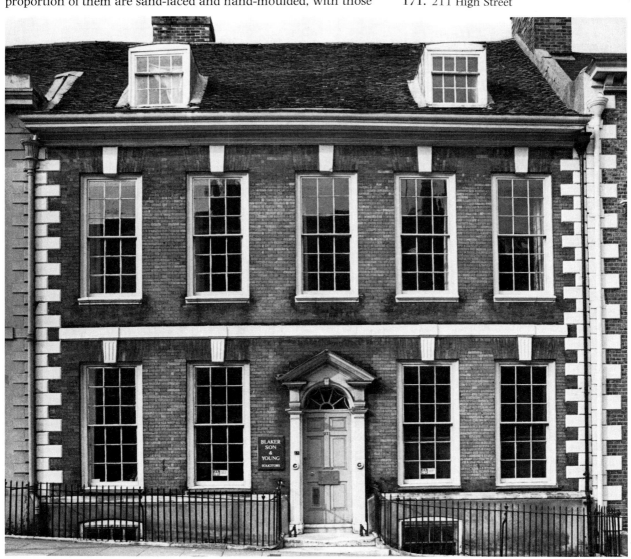

172. 152–155 High Street

slight irregularities and subtle colour variations which add liveliness and interest even to the plainest wall. With Georgian houses, such as 211 High Street (171), meticulously pointed red brick is an excellent foil for white stone, plaster or painted wood dressings: doorcase, window-frames, keystones, quoins, plat-band, cornice.

Yet many of the bricks at Lewes are not red but grey: the greys are another Lewes speciality. They were produced in kilns fired with coppice timber of several different kinds. It was the potash in the wood-smoke that was responsible for the light grey facing, which was confined to one end only of each brick; if they were to become vitrified, the bricks needed also to be in the hottest part of the kiln. Usually the grey walling bricks were employed in combination with reds for the dressings, as on the upper floors of 152–153 High Street (172), a simple example which yet displays, as always with greys, header bond throughout. Stretchers could not be burnt in this way owing to the uneven distribution of heat in the kiln, nor are there any grey M-tiles, for, although these are almost all headers, a thin tile could also not be subjected to so much heat without the risk of distortion.

The grey facing was only skin deep, and sometimes, as at School Hill House (173), it can be seen to have partly worn away. This is one of Lewes's most imposing Georgian houses. The detailing of the first-floor window heads, with their fine cut brickwork, is most accomplished.

An especially satisfying example of Lewes brickwork is Malling House (174), which was formerly the manor house of South Malling, a mile north-east of the town centre. This is a large Queen Anne house, dated 1710, with a dignified roof of sandstone slates. All else is brick, except the windows and the fine wooden doorcase with fluted pilasters in the Doric mode. The bricks are predominantly grey and again, as usual, all headers, but reds were employed for the cornice, the plat-band dividing the ground from the first floor, and the surrounds of the windows; the window-heads have gauged bricks of fine quality. This stately house is now the headquarters of the East Sussex police, who maintain it very well.

The so-called white brick so popular in the first half of the

173. School Hill House, High Street

174. Malling House

175. English's Passage, off Cliffe High Street

176. Priory Crescent, Southover

177. 101 High Street

nineteenth century is not common in Lewes, but Priory Crescent at Southover (*c.* 1835–45) (176) provides an imposing example. In this chalky area the need for plenty of lime in the clay presented no problem.

Bricks were so easy to come by here that they were freely used for paving. Like many old towns, Lewes has kept a number of streets so narrow that they can only be for walkers. These passages have many names: wynds at Richmond in Yorkshire and in Edinburgh; lanes at Tewkesbury and Carlisle; rows at Great Yarmouth as well as at Saffron Walden; scores at Lowestoft; and doubtless there are others. At Lewes they are known as twittens: a delightful word, said to be a corruption of 'betwixt and between'. The illustration (175) shows English's Passage, a twitten opening off Cliffe High Street. Another one, also paved with bricks, is Pipe Passage, near the Castle, named after a clay pipe factory.

Yet, despite the outstanding quality of the local bricks, the yearning in the first half of the nineteenth century for 'a stone look' resulted, as at Chichester, another Sussex town with notably fine Georgian brickwork, in a considerable number of buildings being given an overcoat of stucco. Although smooth now, and rightly so, these stucco fronts, like those in Northgate Street at Warwick (cf. p. 43), are all likely to have been originally covered with a network of carefully incised lines intended to suggest mortar courses, as can still be clearly seen on the upper part of 44 High Street (178). A modest but very gracious example is 101 (177), built with a brick front about the middle of the eighteenth century. Much more imposing, and still in the High Street, is the White Hart Hotel (179), a timber-framed structure originally built as long ago as 1579; later it became one of the town houses of the Pelham family. Needless to say, the rather assertive but very handsome

76

77

stuccoed front was a nineteenth-century addition.

Nearly opposite is stucco in an altogether more original guise. Castle Place (180) was designed in 1810 by Amon Wilds, a builder-cum-architect who a little later was to make an important contribution to the appearance of Brighton. The special feature of this stucco-fronted house, which looks very smart today in its painted brownish-ochre livery, is the pair of pilasters crowned by Ammonite capitals. This fascinating departure from the usual Classical Orders was in fact invented by George Dance the Younger for a building erected in Pall Mall, London, in 1789. Big scrolly fossil ammonites certainly make excellent volutes. Antony Dale has suggested, very plausibly, surely, that Amon Wilds and his son Amon Henry were probably first attracted to what is now sometimes called the 'Ammonite order' by the sheer coincidence of the punning allusion to their Christian names!* What is certain is that they were to introduce it again on at least six occasions in Brighton. This house was bought in 1816 by Dr Gideon Mantell, who was, appropriately enough, a geologist. Whether he was attracted by the ammonite capitals is not recorded, but it seems not unlikely.

The development of fine brickwork in Lewes, and later the vogue for stucco, went hand in hand with the town's prosperity during the eighteenth and early nineteenth centuries, which was really not industrial but social. 'What adds character to this fine, pleasant, well built town,' wrote Daniel Defoe in 1722, 'is that it is full of gentlemen of good families and fortunes, of which the Pelhams may be named with the first. Here are also the ancient families of Gage, Shely [*sic*], &c, formerly Roman but now

*Antony Dale, *Fashionable Brighton, 1820–1860* (1947) p. 26.

180. Castle Place, 166 High Street

Protestant, with many others.' These people had their country houses a few miles out, but they liked also to have secondary houses in the town, where they would come principally to enjoy themselves. A racecourse was laid out as early as 1718; a theatre was built in 1789.

Other occupants of these handsome town houses were professional men, such as doctors and lawyers, and also successful merchants. People such as these required good-looking shops, and happily some still survive. Elphick's (181), in Cliffe High Street – which may be made into a 'walkers only' street: I hope it will, for it is much too narrow for traffic – goes back to the eighteenth century, although the handsome colonnade of Tuscan Doric columns consorts somewhat uneasily, it has to be admitted, with the typically Victorian frilly tile-hanging above.

Up the hill, in Lewes High Street, is a specially enjoyable sequence: numbers 43 to 48. Not all the bow windows are old, but the front of 44 (178) goes back to the early nineteenth century and is notable for its intricate wrought-iron cornice, with vine leaves. A few yards lower down, at 35, is one of those pretty cast-iron balconies with the anthemion or honeysuckle pattern, produced locally by John Every's foundry (later the Phoenix Ironworks) at about the same time. Others are to be seen on a terrace of pleasing Regency houses close by, in Albion Street.

The nineteenth century in Lewes was a flourishing time for brewing. By 1823 the town had no fewer than five breweries.

181. 18 Cliffe High Street

Harvey and Son and Beard and Co. are the only firms that survive. The former (which now does all the brewing for both) was founded in 1790. In 1880 the original Georgian brewery was rebuilt, and its rather attractive Victorian tower in red brick now dominates the lower part of the town (182). The architect, William Bradford, specialised in breweries: examples of his work can also be seen at Frant, Hook Norton in Oxfordshire and Cheltenham.

Until recently the great problem at Lewes, as in almost every other old English town, was the traffic. But here it is good to be able to say that the situation is not nearly as bad as it was. In 1967 the Roads and Bridges committee of the East Sussex County Council submitted a scheme for an inner relief road which would have done irreparable harm to the town and which understandably provoked intense local resistance. Fortunately it was turned down. Since then the southern by-pass has been built, an excellent road which destroys no amenities, and recently the tunnel over a quarter of a mile long under Malling Hill has greatly relieved the situation on the east side of the town. It is really only the traffic from the London direction via Chailey that still poses a problem. Road improvements on the north side of the town would be the best answer, to keep all but local traffic out of the High Street.

Lewes has for me a twofold appeal. There is the old town itself, bestraddling its chalky crest and spilling down the slopes (183), with its abundant legacy of flint, tiles and brick. And then there is the setting, of which surely the fortunate citizens never grow tired: that glorious Downland landscape with the clean lines of the hills silhouetted against the sky.

182. Harvey's Brewery

183. View from Cliffe, looking west

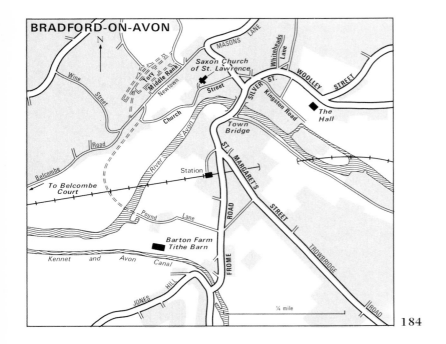

185. Saxon Church of St Lawrence from the
north-east, Holy Trinity Church in the background

5. Bradford-on-Avon

Bradford is in Wiltshire, but Somerset is only two miles away. (This, incidentally, is the part of Somerset which our masters tell us we must now call Avon, but not everyone obeys.) And if the main chain of the Cotswolds reaches its southernmost end above Bath, an outlier stretches to Bradford. The Avon provides the final punctuation mark for both. The derivation is from the old British word *abona*, meaning river; but this Avon is no relation of the one we encountered at Warwick.

This town has easily the longest history of the six in this book, for it is known that by about 500 BC an early Iron Age tribe was entrenched on Budbury Hill, a mile north-west of today's town centre. The settlement covered about six acres and was supplied with water from a spring on the hilltop. The hill falls steeply to the south-east and south-west, and between, on a south-facing spur, was Budbury Castle, an earthwork protected by a double ring of ditches, which overlooks the Avon. Some of the pottery excavated here a few years ago was found to be Roman and even later, so there can be no doubt that the Romans were here too. The Saxons arrived about 650, at a time when the valley was still marshy and undrained. There was no bridge. It was at this time that occur the first references to Bradanforda. Here is the origin of the town's name: Broad ford.

Within a generation the Saxons had established a monastery here, but with this the Saxon church of St Lawrence, which may, I suppose, be Bradford's best know building, would not seem to have been connected. This little church, which is only 38 feet 4 inches long and 13 feet 2 inches wide, but built of stone, has had an extraordinary history. Probably dating from the tenth century, it would appear to have dropped out of use after the erection of the first parish church of the Holy Trinity, a few yards away, about the middle of the twelfth century. From that time onwards it gradually became so hemmed in by other buildings, and altered internally, that its very existence was forgotten. Like other Saxon churches, it was very high in proportion to its area: the chancel 18 feet, the nave 25 feet 3 inches. This made it possible to divide the building horizontally. The chancel arch was walled up, and later removed, to make room for a chimney stack. The nave was converted into a two-storeyed building, with ordinary domestic windows and a door inserted in the west wall. Upstairs there was a school room, accessible by a staircase in the north, and only surviving, *porticus* (a kind of primitive transept). The ground floor was in due course turned into the school kitchen. Meanwhile the chancel had become a quite independent cottage, with no fewer than three storeys and, again, Georgian windows. The disguise was enhanced by a great profusion of ivy.

The vicar of Bradford in 1857, Canon Jones, happened to be an enthusiastic archaeologist. In that year, during some internal repairs, two angels carved in shallow relief were revealed, facing

186. St Lawrence's Church from the south-west

187. Barton Farm Tithe Barn, north side

inwards into a wall. The blocks of stone had evidently been reused. This gave the vicar his clue, but another fourteen years were to elapse before the owners of this property were finally bought out. So it was not until the 1870s that this little church could at last be revealed (185, 186). A great deal of restoration was of course necessary. The south *porticus*, which had long disappeared, was rightly not replaced. But the west wall had to be entirely rebuilt, while, within, a new chancel arch was required, a new wooden roof for the nave, and much else. So, as the photographs show, the church is now a patchwork of old and new, and perhaps of more value historically than aesthetically. The two flying angels, restored to their correct positions in the walls flanking the chancel arch (which they face, and from which no doubt was once suspended, between them, a rood or crucifix), are unfortunately so high up that they cannot easily be seen.

By the beginning of the twelfth century, the Saxon monastery had already been dissolved, but in 1001 it had been granted by King Ethelred to the nuns of Shaftesbury, and the nunnery remained Bradford's landowner throughout the Middle Ages. The town was a most valuable possession, on account of the wool trade.

Three words tell us nearly all that need be known about Bradford's industrial history: wool, stone, and rubber. This town, though never large, has enjoyed long periods of prosperity, and those three industries have held the key to it. Rubber did not appear on the scene until the middle of the nineteenth century. Until then the story is dominated by the other two.

Wool came first, and was the staple industry of Bradford for more than six hundred years: from the time of Henry II to that of George IV. Geography helps to explain why. For not many miles to the south-east lies the perimeter of Salisbury Plain: the chalk downs of Wiltshire, not good for arable, but excellent for pasture. 'They are all hilly,' wrote Daniel Defoe in 1724, 'spreading themselves far and wide, in plains and grassy downs, for breeding and feeding vast flocks of sheep: a prodigious number of them. . . . The first planters of the clothing manufacture doubtless chose this delightful vale [of the Avon] for its seat because of the neighbourhood of those plains.'

There could be no more striking indication of the flourishing state of the wool trade than the fact that by the middle of the fourteenth century the Abbess of Shaftesbury needed Barton Farm tithe barn. She was presiding over the richest nunnery in the country, and the magnificent barn (189), 168 feet long and therefore bigger than many churches, was primarily required for the storage of fleeces. Ecclesiastical landlords were in the, for them. fortunate situation of being legally entitled to a tenth part of the produce of their tenants' farms, and barns went up all over the country – though few were as grand as this one – to accommodate these tithes. Today this barn is, very properly, a national possession under the care of the Department of the Environment.

Outside, except for the doors at the entrance to what might be

188. Barton Farm Tithe Barn, interior

189. Barton Farm Tithe Barn, south side

called the transepts (the technical word is 'streys'), all is limestone. The walls are built of the local oolitic stone, one of the group known generically as Bath stone. But this stone is not naturally fissile: that is to say, it cannot easily be split into thin slices along the bedding planes. So for the roof, which called for stone slates – or stone tiles, as some people prefer to call them – in their thousands, at an unusually steep pitch, the builders had to look elsewhere. They did not have to go far. These stone slates, which are one of the great sights of Bradford, come from the formation known to geologists as the Forest Marble; and probably from near Atworth, which is about four miles to the north-east. As with all stone roofs before the nineteenth century, the slates are laid in courses of gradually diminishing size from the broadest at the eaves to the narrowest at the ridge.

The streys are a good deal larger and more prominent on the north side (187), which faces towards the town. The masonry is of the finest quality, with large blocks and very assured details, such as the set-offs (sloping ledges) to protect the many buttresses, the coping on the gables, and the ornamental finials.

Within (188), the great thrill is the tremendously massive oak roof spanning a width of 33 feet. The roof is arch-braced, with no fewer than three tiers of wind-braces along the entire length under the purlins (the name for the beams which run longitudinally at intervals below the ridge-beam). It will be readily appreciated that, by comparison with this grand piece of medieval masoncraft and carpentry, the Saxon church, although better known, offers no aesthetic experience that is in the least comparable.

Up the hill on the opposite (north) side of the river was the Priory, which also had its tithe barn (190). This fell into decay, but in recent years has been rescued and reconditioned by the very active local Preservation Society. Part of it now serves as a meeting hall; the rest is a small private house. There are some pretty late-medieval windows and another richly textured stone-slated roof. Inside the house is a good plaster ceiling retrieved some years ago by the Society from Merchant's Barton, a house in Frome, and installed here with great skill. The date of the ceiling, 1658, is by no means contemporary with its new setting, but it looks well enough and was certainly worth preserving. Frome's loss has been Bradford's gain.

190. Priory Barn

At first the fleeces were sold to be worked upon elsewhere, but before the end of the fourteenth century a cloth-making industry had been established in the town itself. Along the banks of the river arose a succession of cloth mills, for which the water provided the power; at length, by the beginning of the nineteenth century, there were no fewer than thirty-two of them. The requirement was for between two and three million fleeces a year. For these they looked originally to the Wiltshire downs, but when some of this land was given over to corn-growing they had to turn to London, where so-called Kentish wool was available, and also to the Midlands and North. Well before then the Bradford cloth trade had become highly organised. For the spinning and weaving of narrow cloth the wool was despatched on horseback to the surrounding villages; until the Industrial Revolution this was a cottage industry. The riders returned with some of the spun yarn, ready now for the looms. In the town itself they wove broadcloths (which required much bigger looms, up to 100 inches wide). These heavy felted cloths of very fine quality acquired an international reputation in the eighteenth century. All the finishing and dyeing of the cloths was also undertaken at Bradford.

This story ended with the erection in the nineteenth century of the two largest mills of them all. Kingston Mill, seen on the left in a watercolour of c. 1850 (191), was built by Thomas Divett in 1811. As a mill it was a commercial failure but, as we shall see, it had

191. Kingston Mill and the Hall, *c.* 1850

another role to play, and survived until 1972. The other, Abbey Mill (192), did not go up until 1875. It was a brave but unsuccessful attempt to revive at Bradford a nearly moribund industry: its very last fling, anywhere in the West Country. On one occasion the workers took a voluntary reduction in wages to help keep the mill going. But at last it too had to change its function. In 1968–72 it was converted into offices and a restaurant. It is a handsome edifice, with a frieze of little arches, pointed and corbelled, below the cornice and the parapet, and all built of the local stone.

Another reminder of the wool trade is the old rug factory up on Budbury Hill, prominent on the skyline in plate 3. This became an engineering works, and is now being tactfully converted for residential use. (There is a preservation order on the front of the building.)

The original broad ford was replaced in the thirteenth century by a narrow pack-horse bridge of nine arches, of which two can still be seen on the east side of the present bridge. A glance at the plan (184) will suffice to show that the bridge was, and still is, the hub of the town: all the principal streets converge on it.

As not infrequently in the Middle Ages, the bridge carried a small chapel, for which, near the centre, there is an exceptionally broad pier. The other piers have, facing upstream, sturdy cutwaters. In the latter part of the seventeenth century the bridge was widened considerably, and most of the arches were rebuilt. This is the bridge

192. Abbey Mill

193. The Town Bridge

194. 7–8 The Shambles

which we see today (193). By then the chapel had been rebuilt as a lock-up, square with a domed roof, also of stone, crowned by a characteristically seventeenth-century finial, bearing aloft a copper-gilt weathervane in the form of a fish: the Bradford Gudgeon. This grim little building can still be inspected. It contains an entrance lobby and two tiny cells, with iron bedsteads fixed to the dividing wall. With the river flowing directly underneath, the lavatories presented no problem. After ceasing to be used for prisoners, it became for a while an ammunition store.

In medieval times, in Bradford as in nearly every other English town, a good many buildings, of the humbler kind especially, were timber-framed, but survivors here are very scarce. Two little houses in the Shambles (194) could date from about 1500, although later a good deal altered. The present shop-fronts are Victorian and the roof tiles are modern. Although not un-picturesque, they hardly seem to 'belong' here. And the reason is that the whole town stands on stone. As early as 1540 Leland was able to record that 'the towne is made all of stone'.

Until the Industrial Revolution, the great factor inhibiting the use of heavy materials like stone for house building was the cost of transport. But at Bradford this did not apply. Its hills are honeycombed with quarry workings, most of them shallow mines, which can go in as much as a mile. Their rather precarious roofs have been known to fall in. None of the town's quarries is any longer worked for stone. They can, however, serve other purposes. For more than a hundred years some have been used for growing mushrooms. One of the major producers in the country – who grows more than twelve million tons of them a year! – now operates here, giving full-time employment to about eighty people. The worked-out quarries available for mushroom growing cover an area of some twenty-five acres. But production is mainly centred upon two large ones which are used alternately: while one is being filled with the new crop, the other is being emptied for sterilisation. Nearly a hundred tons of fresh stable manure are needed every week.

Stone, even on the site, was more expensive to use than wood, although as a building material it presented far fewer problems here than in most English towns. But it was not all good stone, even though it was oolitic limestone. It is not uncommon to find stonework in perfect preservation and adjacent blocks in varying states of decay on the same house (204).

The non-fissile character of the local oolite, referred to earlier, has also done Bradford a disservice. Stone slates from the Forest Marble, such as were used on the tithe barns, continued to be laid on certain roofs, as at the Old Manor House (196), but more often the easier and cheaper course, of resorting to tiles, has been followed. Red roofing tiles never look good on a stone house, and in any general view of this town the one inharmonious note, visually, is the profusion of red roofs, which consort ill with the limestone.

Although not right here, the pantiles from Bridgwater are certainly the most acceptable, and Bradford can show quite a lot of

195. 10–14 Barton Orchard

196. Old Manor House, Whiteheads Lane

195

196

these. Pantiles, as I have already indicated (cf. p. 60), are far commoner in the eastern and especially in the north-eastern parts of England than in the west, with the sole exception of the area around Bridgwater, which from the later eighteenth century became one of our principal centres of production for this kind of tile. Hence there are plenty of pantiles in Somerset, and on the Avon and its tributaries they were carried into north-west Wiltshire.

Some of the modern machine-produced tiles are really very unattractive indeed: harsh in colour and texture, and often niggling in design. Bradford has all too many of them. Concrete tiles are generally better designed, but also machine-made, unpleasing in texture, and tend to look dingy after a few years. (In this respect, it is said that the recent products are better. Time alone will show.) If for financial reasons an artificial product has to be used, Bradstone or similar slates, as seen on the north (back) side of the Old Manor House, are very much to be preferred. These are right in colour for a limestone house, and graded in the traditional manner.

By the Georgian period many, probably most, of Bradford's cloth workers were living in stone houses. An interesting survivor is Barton Orchard (195), built as a terrace for cloth workers with the houses divided horizontally. This presented no problem, for the terrace is sited on a steep hillside, so that the two upper storeys could be entered at ground level from the back. The grouping of many of the windows in pairs might almost be termed a Bradford speciality: many of them served workrooms, in which a good light was essential. In the early part of the present century this terrace fell into a state of dilapidation, from which, however, about twenty years ago it was fortunately rescued and converted into five very good houses.

Higher up the hill, in what is called Middle Rank, is a pleasing range of houses, some gabled. These were built in 1697, also originally for cloth workers. In recent years they have been carefully reconstructed and most of them are now council houses. Thence we can climb again, by steps, to the narrow street, for walkers only, known as Tory – or formerly, rather delightfully, as Top Rank Tory. This, I hasten to add, had absolutely no connection with the upper echelons of the Conservative party. Its name derives from *tor*, meaning a high place. (Think of Glastonbury Tor. And Dartmoor is studded with *tors*). What were once workers' cottages stand alongside Georgian terrace houses. Although they command an extensive view, the hill still climbs precipitously behind them. So much so, in fact, that a few of the houses still have back kitchens in caves hewn out of the limestone cliff.

The top men, the master clothiers, were often very well housed indeed. Most of their houses are Georgian, but the Old Manor House (196), already twice referred to for its roof, looks a little earlier, and the part on the right, only glimpsed in the photograph, goes back to the seventeenth century. The windows, no doubt, were originally casements: their proportions are a little too wide for

197. Well Close House

Georgian, hence the four lights across and four up, instead of the usual three by four. Such slender glazing bars as these are unlikely to be earlier than the end of the eighteenth century. They are absolutely vital to the good appearance of the house.

The effect may be compared with that of Well Close House (197), which is also of two dates; this is a seventeenth-century house which was given a fine new front in the first part of the eighteenth century. In the Victorian period the glazing bars of the downstairs windows were removed, no doubt with the idea that it would improve the views of the garden. What a price to pay! The

198. Kingston House

masonry, on the other hand, is most distinguished. The upper part, including the pediment which stretches over the whole width of the building, is entirely ashlar: that is to say, of sawn blocks, squared and finely jointed in level courses. The first floor is the grandest, with moulded architraves, moulded sills supported on curved stone brackets, and pediments over every window, alternately segmental and triangular. To compensate for this, the ground floor, like the quoins, is wholly rusticated; the recessing of the joints between each big block of stone was a well-tried device in classical architecture for endowing the base storey of a building with an appearance of greater weight and authority. The bull's-eye window in the pediment, also within a strongly moulded frame, is good too.

Another device of Georgian architecture, much heavier than rustication but undoubtedly making an impact, was used for the central doorway at Kingston House (198). The alternate stones of which the Tuscan columns are here composed have been 'blocked', and so have the alternate voussoirs of the arched doorhead, including the keystone. This deliberately broken surface, with emphatic contrasts of light and shade, is in striking contrast to the smooth ashlar of the rest of the front, the urbanity of which is also different from the crude rubblestone of the side-wall, which plays no part in the architectural ensemble nor was intended to. The modern tiled roof is also a poor thing which, however, does not impinge very much. But violence has been done to this handsome Georgian front in two other ways which could easily be corrected. There is, again, the removal of the glazing bars on the ground floor, a particular inanity in this instance as there is no garden to be viewed. The bars could be replaced at comparatively little cost but with enormous improvement to the appearance of the building. Even worse is the effect of the creeper – to which I would not object on the rubblestone side-wall: that would be a good place for it. But apart from the doorway, this façade, although an excellent piece of masoncraft, is decidely plain: the only other 'features' are the boldy projecting triangular pediments over the two end windows of the ground floor. At present one of these is so completely masked by the *Ampelopsis veitchii* as to be completely invisible for five months of the year, which really is an affront to the architecture. This ridiculous creeper could, and should, be removed in an afternoon. As Kingston House is now offices, I am hopeful that by the time most people read these words they will already be out of date.

At Westbury House the missing glazing bars on the ground floor were put back quite recently, and since this house is very conspicuously sited just across the Town Bridge, thousands of people must have felt grateful to the new owners; now divided into six flats, it looks almost unbelievably better than it used to. The work of restoration has been of a uniformly high standard. And how timely: for this early Georgian house is one of Bradford's finest. The south front (200) is a design of great assurance, which is as it should be, for it faces directly up St Margaret's Street, the principal approach road to the town from the south. Horizontally the string courses grow bolder at each stage, to culminate in a very strong cornice surmounted by an open balustrade. Vertically the enrichment is concentrated on the central bay. In front there is an array of big stone balls in acanthus leaf cups, standing on rusticated stone piers. The east front, facing the garden, is also a work of distinction. This house was the birthplace, in 1800, of a future Lord Chancellor. Richard Bethell became Lord Westbury, which is why it bears its present name.

In a letter of 1724, Defoe wrote: 'They told us at Bradford that it was no extraordinary thing to have clothiers worth from ten to forty thousand pounds a man [large sums in those days] and many of the great families who now pass for gentry have been originally raised from, and built up by, this truly noble manufacture.' No wonder they wanted to be well housed, particularly in an age when one's house was the great status symbol.

Yet none of these clothiers' houses was designed by an architect, as we understand the word today. At the beginning of the eighteenth century, architects were still few and far between. It was the master-builders who were responsible; and, in addition to

199. Church House, 29 Church Street

200. Westbury House, south front

long apprenticeship, they learned in two ways: by studying the numerous manuals and pattern books which were then becoming available, and by looking – looking at the houses of their colleagues, or maybe rivals, and often trying, no doubt, to improve upon them.

With Westbury House it is interesting to compare Druce's Hill House (201), which is also an early Georgian building of fine quality. Although there are variations of detail, the overall affinity between them will be immediately apparent, and as works of art there is little to choose between them. It would also be difficult to say which came first; indeed, it is not unlikely that they were the work of the same builder. But there are subtle differences, especially of proportion. Here the rooms are larger in area but not as lofty, so the windows are more amply spaced but not as tall. The greater window area at Westbury House is more lively, especially as the architraves there are fully moulded; here the effect is plainer, but more restful. Both houses have some windows with curved heads. Here the quoins are more emphatic, because they are rusticated. The balustrade – as on the east side of Westbury House, not illustrated – has open balusters only over the windows; but at

201. Druce's Hill House, 22 Church Street

202. Silver Street House

203. Audley's, 5 Woolley Street

the centre this balustrade curves up a little, a nice touch. The clients here were two brothers: Anthony and William Druce. Both were Quakers, and both were clothiers. Behind this affluent-looking front, part of the house is older.

At Church House (199), which dates from 1731 but was not given its name until the nineteenth century, the great feature is the Venetian window, a work of exquisite accomplishment, with Ionic pilasters and a richly moulded architrave which, as so often in eighteenth-century houses, lights the hall and the staircase. The whole of the central part of this façade, which is crowned by a pediment, steps forward a little; and by rusticating the ground-floor quoins of this portion of the house, as well as the arched frame of the doorway, the Venetian window is provided with a sort of plinth, of splendid strength.

The client at Silver Street House (202), also early Georgian, was again a prosperous clothier. This design lacks the elegance of the foregoing, but is certainly imposing. The four small arched windows are dummies. Built on a hill in a narrow, crowded street, this house presently lost its attraction as a residence and became an inn: The Bear. By 1974 it was derelict, and would probably have been demolished had not the local Preservation Society again intervened. By dint of much unselfish work sufficient funds were raised to save it, and the Society has been responsible for an admirable piece of reconditioning. Unlike all the other clothiers' houses which I have been describing, this one was not originally faced with ashlar. The rubblestone walls were therefore rendered and painted. The present stone facing is quite a recent addition.

Farther up the hill, especially in Woolley Street which is a continuation of Silver Street, there are several more of these handsome clothiers' houses: too many to be discussed here. I select just two of them, Sundial House (204) and Audley's (203), the latter with a portico of the Tuscan order. Both these houses have the paired windows referred to earlier. In other respects, however, they are not quite as grand as those already described.

Belcombe Court, on the other hand, which in the eighteenth century was known as Belcombe Brook Villa, is still grander (205). Situated just outside the town to the west, this is the finest of all the clothiers' houses, and the most unexpected. Clothing was manufactured on this site before the end of the Middle Ages, and the still existing (though much restored) barn dates from that time. The Yerbury family were already prominent as Bradford clothiers under the Tudors. When they came here is not known exactly, but the way into the entrance court is through the archway on the right of plate 205. This is surmounted by a circular stone turret, dome and cupola which, although undated, could belong to the very beginning of the eighteenth century. It served at one time as a dovecot, and still has its nesting boxes.

Then, in 1734, Francis Yerbury decided to add on a new Palladian wing, and here, for the first time in the history of the clothiers' houses, an established architect steps upon the scene; none other than John Wood the elder, of Bath, the leading architect of the

West country at this time. Wood certainly did his client proud, in every sense of the word, for a proud building this is, wearing an air of tremendous authority, with a large modillioned pediment rising above a strong architrave carried on smooth Ionic pilasters. The pediment culminates in a trio of garlanded stone urns. Wood himself, never one to take a despairing view of his own abilities, declared the frontispiece to be 'the best that hath yet been executed in or about Bath'.

The stone was Bradford's best. For, of all the quarries in or close to the town, only one, Westwood, yielded stone of a quality equal, or nearly equal, to the top range of the Bath products and, as luck would have it, this quarry, although on the other side of the river, is only about a mile from Belcombe. Westwood can be distinguished from the other Bath limestones by the presence, here and there, of small brownish flecks, which are nodules of iron. They are not really blemishes: it might in fact be held that they add interest.

The Palladian wing has two specially fine rooms. The study is masterly: a small and lofty octagon, with exquisite woodcarving round the windows, on the shutters, and above the two niches made for the display of china. But the showpiece is the plasterwork of the ceiling (207). Graceful swags of leaves, rosebuds and grapes adorn the cove, to culminate at the centre in a design of six rollicking *putti* or cherubs, perched upon clouds and encircling a basketful of fruit and flowers, magically suspended. Who these excellent craftsmen were is not known: it seems not unlikely that

204. Sundial House, 13 Whiteheads Lane

205. Belcombe Court from the south-west

206. Belcombe Court garden

the plasterer was an Italian. The adjoining room is what Wood called the parlour: it is now the drawing room. This has equally exuberant woodcarving which is undoubtedly by the same man, but the plasterwork is somewhat different and not so memorable. It is, however, easy to enjoy the butterflies that flutter unexpectedly across the ceiling.

Where Belcombe Court differs strikingly from all the other clothiers' houses is in the extent of the private grounds, which have survived virtually unchanged for nearly 250 years. On a fairly modest scale, they are an almost perfect example of the landscape style of William Kent: a precious survival, therefore, of what the French termed *le jardin anglais* (206). There are a serpentine pool, a grotto, a Doric *tempietto* on a knoll, a rustic cottage – perhaps here recalling the original dwellings of the clothiers – and a beautifully undulating park with trees artfully clumped. For this is, needless to say, the art that conceals art: the naturalness was in fact all most carefully contrived.

The Yerburys continued to inhabit Belcombe Court until the beginning of the present century. Lucky people.

The heyday of Bradford's cloth trade lasted for about 150 years: from *c.* 1660 to *c.* 1810. Then the situation altered. Bradford's broad cloth, as has been observed, was of fine quality but heavy. Early in the nineteenth century taste changed in favour of much lighter worsted cloths, and these were provided, not by Wiltshire,

207. Belcombe Court, ceiling of study

208. Avoncliff Aqueduct, west side

but by the Yorkshire mills. They produced cheap cloth, making use of torn-up rags, which the West of England scorned to its cost. The process of decline was hastened by the recession which accompanied and followed the war against Napoleon. It soon became necessary for Bradford people to find another means of subsistence.

This was provided, for a while, by the stone industry. The stone, of course, had been there all the time: vast quantities of it. With only one small exception it is the material of every building so far described. But the ever-present problem was transport. In the eighteenth century navigation on the Avon was improved, at a time when the only way of carrying for any distance a heavy material like stone was still by barge. It was the opening of the Kennet and Avon Canal (3) in 1810 which changed the situation entirely. This canal first made it feasible to despatch Bath stone on much longer journeys, and, in particular, to London. In this trade Bradford had its share. Then, in the 1850s, the railway arrived to share the valley with the river and the canal, and, ultimately, to put the latter out of business. The transport situation was still further improved. The local stone could be sent all over Britain. Before the end of the century there were sixteen stone quarries in operation in the neighbourhood of Bradford. In the Winsley quarries alone, work had been provided for more than a hundred men.

Most of these quarries were mines, but that does not imply that there were shafts. At many of them the 'roads' were kept almost level as they burrowed into the hillsides. That is the situation at Westwood, the only one of the Bradford quarries that is still working – and even here there was a long period of closure. This stone has already been described in connection with Belcombe Court. It is owing to the remarkable technological advances made by the stone industry in recent years that this excellent quarry could be reopened. At the quarry face, which is at present about 300 yards from the entrance, a stone-cutting machine does in one hour what used to take a man a fortnight of very hard labour. I saw, loaded on a trailer, a single block of stone which weighed nearly four tons. Westwood stone has lately been used, for example, in the restoration of Dorchester Abbey in Oxfordshire.

The other local quarries, as has been said, could not compete. Some of their stone was really indifferent. A prize example, ironically enough, is on the very canal which was partly built to carry the local limestone. In the four-mile stretch of the Kennet and Avon Canal to the west of Bradford two aqueducts had to be built to carry it over the Avon. Both were the work of the great bridge-builder John Rennie; both are massive structures with triple arches. The Dundas Aqueduct near Limpley Stoke is still a majestic sight. Not so the Avoncliff Aqueduct (208), which is much closer to Bradford. Here the canal is at present dry and its bed choked with vegetation, but it is hoped before long to restore it. The stone for this bridge was obtained in 1803 from a quarry a few hundred yards away which was opened specially. It could hardly have been worse selected. Only the parapets, which came from different beds, have proved more durable.

So the stone industry, although much better than nothing, was unable, at Bradford, to provide a total replacement for the loss of the clothmaking. In the 1830s and 1840s the town was no longer at all prosperous. The stage was therefore set for the arrival of the most remarkable man in the history of Bradford: Stephen Moulton (1794–1880) (209). He was a paradigm of the successful Victorian businessman; enterprising, self-confident, prepared to take risks, and immensely industrious. Born in Devon of a family of seafarers, he had, about 1835, gone to work in New York, where he had encountered Charles Goodyear, the discoverer of how to vulcanise rubber. In due course, Moulton obtained the British patent for this process, and, having failed to interest the Government in it, he determined to become a rubber manufacturer himself. With next to no capital he needed backers, and one of those who responded was his friend Captain Palairet, who lived at Woolley Grange, a seventeenth-century house a mile north-east of Bradford. He assured him that there he would be able to find not only the labour, but even a factory. And so it was that he acquired, in 1846, Divett's empty cloth mill (191), which he quickly adapted. The essence of Goodyear's invention was the conversion of rubber in its natural state, a gum gathered in little cups from the trunks of innumerable rubber trees, into a material at once strong and elastic, by adding sulphur and subjecting it to a very high temperature. In America itself conditions were not yet ripe for the industrial exploitation of rubber, so the inventor was quite willing to grant Moulton the necessary licence. Manufacture started in 1848 and went ahead by leaps and bounds; within a few years Moulton was supplying thousands of waterproof capes for the Army fighting in the Crimea.

209. Stephen Moulton

210. The Hall and the Rubber Factory. Painting by Tristram Hillier, 1952

Among other very important clients were the railways, who needed rubber parts in large numbers for their rolling stock, especially for buffer springs. Even in dentistry the invention of vulcanised rubber brought about changes of the most far-reaching character. Gone for ever were poor George Washington's wooden dentures! Markets were opened up far beyond the shores of Britain, and today, although no longer controlled by the Moulton family, the Avon Rubber Group is still the principal employer of labour at Bradford. Economically, the advent of this new industry, established in 1848, was the town's means of salvation.

Both the watercolour of *c.* 1850 (191) and Tristram Hillier's oil painting of 1952 (210) show the close proximity of the mill to the large house now known as the Hall. This had been called the Great House, and then Kingston House, after it was inherited in 1722 by an eleven-year-old boy who, four years later, was to succeed his grandfather as the second Duke of Kingston. It was not long before Stephen Moulton bought this too. At the time it was described by the editor of Aubrey's *Natural History of Wiltshire* as 'woefully degraded and mutilated', but because part of it had long been in use as a wool store, it was, luckily, not quite ruinous. It had been the finest house in Bradford, and, thanks to the Moultons, it is so once again. It is also the one large house here not directly dependent for its existence upon a clothing fortune. The family responsible for it, whose name (coincidentally enough) was Hall, had been clothiers. John Hall, who died in 1515, owned five mills here, three of which were for the beating and cleansing of cloth: what is called fulling. But by the time that this house was built they had already become 'gentry' and landowners. Their mills were let out. They had made good marriages.

The last John Hall, who died in 1711, founded, eleven years earlier, in Frome Road, the Almshouses (211), which carry the family coat of arms – three poleaxes – over the door. The roof is a delight. And so are the outsize stone balls on the gate piers. Here too the tradition has been maintained by the incoming family: in 1891 the almshouse was restored and re-endowed by Stephen Moulton's eldest son Horatio.

The Hall (214) was probably built between 1598 and 1601 near, or perhaps on the site of, an earlier house, and even at a very showy moment for English domestic architecture it stands out as a spectacular piece of display. Although there is no documentation, it is believed to be by the leading Elizabethan architect, Robert Smythson, who had already built Wollaton Hall in Nottinghamshire and had in the previous year (1597) completed Hardwick Hall in Derbyshire. The garden front, even more than at Hardwick, does appear to be 'more glass than wall'. In one important feature the Hall goes beyond any of these: the introduction of lobed bows in the centre of the bays on both sides. There were a few early Tudor precedents for these, of which the outstanding surviving example is the still more thrilling cinquefoil oriel at Thornbury Castle in Gloucestershire; but these lobed bows were a glorious extravagance. In other respects the analogies are with Longleat, which is under twenty miles away and was where Smythson worked in his

211. Hall's Almshouses, Frome Road

212. The Hall, east front

213. The Hall, west front, across the Bowling Green lawn

early manhood as the master-mason. The very elaborate ornamentation seems principally to have been inspired by that house, which can also show, for example, inset circles between the two tiers of windows and, as a cresting for the three bays, bigger pierced circles carrying, and flanked by, spear-head finials. Here, though, there are gables too, with more finials; it could hardly be more exuberant.

The stone for this house came from Combe Quarry, a mine in the grounds not more than three hundred yards away. Like a lot of stone in this area, it can be ashlared and, especially when first hewn, is quite easy to carve. For the east side of the house (212), which was originally the service side, they were content to use only rubblestone for the walling material. But the residential side looking on to the bowling green to the west (213), like the 'show' south front, was faced entirely with ashlar.

And since these are the two faces of the house most exposed to the weather, it is certain that the stonework, on the south front especially, was in a fairly bad state of decay when Stephen Moulton

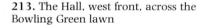

214. The Hall, south front

215. The Hall, the study

acquired the property in 1848. With only one or two variations
(such as the three fleurs-de-lis standing on the scrolls over the
south door, an unconvincing addition), he had everything copied
with punctilious accuracy. That the garden front is now very
largely a Victorian reproduction, and the west side partly so, is
entirely due to the relative lack of strength of this good-looking
stone. But Moulton went to the same quarry again; and after 130
years I challenge anyone who did not know about the refacing to
find any substantial reason for doubting that this house is a
product, and indeed a masterpiece, of the closing years of
Elizabeth I.

The delightful garden is largely Stephen Moulton's creation. The
terrace and the balustrade are mostly original, and so is the
bowling green, or at any rate the part nearer to the house. But
Moulton and his second son John, who succeeded to the property
in 1894, made many improvements, not least the planting of the
surrounding screen of trees which, considering its situation hardly
a quarter of a mile from the town centre, provide the house and
garden with so much seclusion that visitors to Bradford are often

unaware that the Hall is there at all.

Both outside and in, the immense loftiness of the principal rooms is most impressive. But, as at Hardwick Hall, this does mean that the house is not by any means as large as it appears to be, for space is used with prodigal extravagance. Not surprisingly, therefore, Stephen Moulton had a mezzanine floor inserted on the north side of the building, which involved making a new staircase to accommodate the changed levels. Only two rooms have kept their original panelling: the two at the south-east corner, where the wool, for so long stored in them, acted as an excellent preservative. Both rooms have fluted pilasters, Corinthian in what is today the study (215) and Ionic in the room above, with broad and very handsome cornices. Several stone chimney-pieces survive, of which the study has one, and on the strength of similarities in design with a number of others in the south-western counties, including one at Montacute, Arthur Oswald was able to identify the mason as almost certainly William Arnold of Charlton Musgrove near Wincanton.

The study is one of the rooms with the lobed bow window, and it is a delightful experience to sit there looking sideways along the house's sparkling front. The matching room at the south-west corner, now the dining-room, has attractive murals by Graham Rust, painted between 1972 and 1976. They include a number of friends of the present owner, Dr Alex Moulton, and others specially associated with the house.

It must be emphasised that, although access is often granted to the garden, the house is not open to the public. The reason is that Dr Moulton, a distinguished engineering designer whose name is specially associated with the Moulton bicycle, not only lives here but uses parts of the house as his office. So this remarkable building, which Sir Nikolaus Pevsner described as 'the one nationally major mansion of Bradford', is still very much a going concern. 'I am hopeful,' said Dr Moulton a couple of years ago in an address delivered in London at the Royal Society of Arts, 'that the Engineering Laboratory which I have established in the grounds of my historic house will continue to do useful work for the industrial benefit of the nation, and, in so doing, enable the Hall to be preserved as a living entity into the future.'

Bradford-on-Avon, then, is a working town, but one that is also very preservation-conscious. It has, needless to say, too much traffic, but, rightly, there has been no street widening. Like all the towns described in this book, it can only properly be seen by exploration on foot; but the distances are quite small. For lovers of architecture the place provides a visual banquet, starting with the grand Tithe Barn and ending with the splendidly renovated Hall, with the tiny resurrected Saxon church as an archaeological *hors d'oeuvre*. But it is the rich Georgian inheritance which supplies the meal's ample main course. Quite un-Georgian in its layout, this compact little town, built of pale yellow limestone on an excitingly hilly site, is a treasury of Georgian delights.

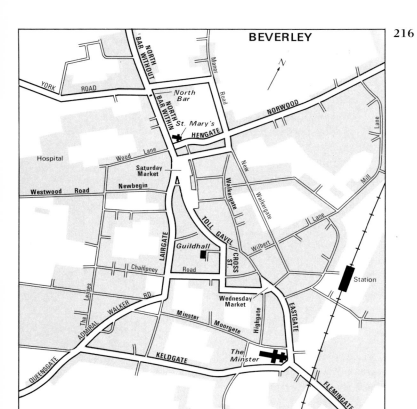

BEVERLEY

216

217. Beverley Minster from the south

6. Beverley

Beverley, having regard to its great artistic importance, must be the least known town in England. In the south I constantly meet people who not only have not visited it, but who have only the haziest idea where it is. 'Somewhere in Yorkshire, isn't it?' they say. 'Yes,' I reply, 'in the East Riding of Yorkshire, eight miles north-west of Hull', ignoring the fact that in 1974 the East Riding, with its immensely long and honourable history, was officially swept into oblivion. Has any piece of legislation within living memory been so insensitive, so insulting even, to deeply felt traditions and loyalties, or so profoundly unpopular? There are a great many people who still long to see it overturned.

Most of the East Riding, including Beverley, was transferred to a new 'county', if with propriety two such disparate bits of ancient counties can be so termed, with the name of Humberside. Most of this 'county', needless to say, is not beside the Humber; some of it is nowhere near it. But the widespread unfamiliarity with Beverley is not, of course, connected with changes in the county boundaries. 'The trouble is,' sighed a Beverlonian to me, a trifle wistfully, 'that we are not on the *way* to anywhere'; and even with the opening of the Humber Bridge that is still largely true. Beverley is 'out on a limb'. Had it not been, it would undoubtedly have been preferred to Ripon in 1836 as Yorkshire's second cathedral city, for its minster is much finer than Ripon's. It is a town which certainly deserves a wider recognition. So this chapter will be not only the last but also the longest.

The early history of the place is nebulous. It now seems certain that there was no Roman settlement here. Its original name was Deira, and from the beginning of the eighth century it harboured a monastic settlement founded by John, fourth Bishop of York, an older contemporary of the Venerable Bede of Jarrow, whose *Ecclesiastical History of the English Nation* provides such a valuable picture of the country in the seventh century. John had been Bishop of Hexham before moving in 705 to York, not yet an Archbishopric. Thirteen years later he retired to his own little monastery, where in 721 he died. His shrine soon came to be venerated, and ultimately, over 300 years later (1037), he was canonised as St John of Beverley.

Meanwhile, about 874, Deira had been wiped out by Viking invaders. When it reappeared, as Beverley, is not known (nor is the origin of the new name), but it was certainly before 938, for in about that year the church was refounded by King Athelstan, as a thankoffering for his victory over the Scots. The dedication was, as it still is, to St John the Evangelist, not to St John the Baptist, nor of course to John of Beverley who was not yet a saint. Like the other two great daughter churches of York, Southwell and Ripon (both now cathedrals), it was to be served not by monks but by a college of secular canons. It was enlarged: during the reign of Edward the

Confessor a big central tower was erected. This stood for about 160 years and then collapsed. Nor was this the only misfortune. On 20 September 1188 (yes, it was September again: cf. page 18) a great fire devastated the town, and the church was badly damaged.

So there is now virtually nothing to be seen at Beverley which is earlier than the thirteenth century. The story then begins in earnest. And here we must start with the churches. This was from the first an ecclestical town. The Archbishop of York was the lord of the manor. To this day the place has not one but two front-rank churches: St John and St Mary. From the fringe of the Wolds to the west their towers, nearly a mile apart, dominate the prospect. From the south, whether the approach be made by road or by rail, only St John is visible, but this view, once seen, is never forgotten. The great edifice is sited at the extreme southern end of the town, with no buildings to mask it. From this direction, which is undoubtedly the best from which to make the approach, it seems to be anchored like a great liner on the level sea of the fields (217).*

St John is always known as the Minster, and of course everyone wants to know why. Alas, it is no use asking me! What does the term signify? The word certainly derives from the Latin, *monasterium*, but, as I have said, it was only in those distant pre-Viking days that there was a monastery here. Westminster, the Minister to the west of the city of London, was a large Benedictine monastery, but otherwise the odd fact is that none of the churches to which the appellation Minster is most often applied – York, Southwell, Howden and Wimborne – was ever monastic. Nor were the cathedrals of Lincoln and Ripon, to which the name is still sometimes given. So it has to be said that the use of this word, mainly confined to the north-east, has never been satisfactorily explained. But it must certainly be kept. I know no lovelier name for a great church.

Yet since 1548 Beverley Minster's status has been no more than that of any other parish church. This is a remarkable fact; for I have no hesitation in saying that, after Westminster Abbey, this is the finest non-cathedral church in the kingdom. Finer than the former abbey churches of Tewkesbury, Sherborne and Selby, finer than the erstwhile priory churches of Great Malvern, Hexham and Christchurch, finer than the parish church of St Mary Redcliffe at Bristol: the seven non-cathedral churches which I would rank next. Superior also to all but about a dozen of the cathedrals. In short, a masterpiece.

When work started on this church, at the east end, about 1235, the stone was obtained from the other side of the Wolds, the hilly range to the west. The quarries, between North Newbald and North Cave, were barely ten miles away as the crow is supposed to fly, but the stone was too heavy to be dragged over these hills, so it had to be hauled down to the Humber and brought thence by

---

* At the time of writing, certain interested parties are doing their utmost to see that this memorable view shall not be wholly preserved. By the time this book is published I hope, although I am not at all confident, that these short-sighted philistines will have been well and truly vanquished.

218. Beverley Minster roofs, looking east

barge.* It is an Oolitic limestone, and at the east end of the church, outside, the tiny ooliths, looking rather like a cod's roe, are quite easy to identify. But fairly soon this stone would seem to have run out, for well before 1300 it gave place to Magnesian limestone, brought all the way from the West Riding: from Huddlestone, near Tadcaster, down the Wharfe, and from Cadeby, near Doncaster, down the Don. Both these rivers flow into the Ouse, which becomes the Humber. And then, to reach Beverley, they had to go up the little river Hull. A quay was constructed within a mile or so of the site. And during the fourteenth century, by deepening and canalising a stream known as the Beck, the barges carrying the stone were brought still nearer. The Magnesian limestone, formerly much used in parts of Yorkshire, is often nearly white, but at Beverley, after cleaning, it has a decidedly yellowish tinge. It is a beautiful stone, but not very tough, so in places there has been a good deal of external decay from weathering.

Compared with those of the Continent, the great English Gothic churches are far less compact. The emphasis is on length rather than width or height. The transepts project considerably, and sometimes, as here, there is a second pair. The design of the church is not, as in France, centripetal, concerned before all else with spatial effects, but centrifugal, spreading outwards in every direction. At the Minster this difference can be specially well appreciated by climbing one of the west towers to view the roofs (218). These are of very steep pitch, and sheathed with lead.

*Pink fire marks suggest that some of this Newbald stone may have come from an earlier church on the site. (Information from Dr Ivan Hall.)

219. Beverley Minster, the south and south-east transepts

It is not my intention to describe either of Beverley's churches in any great detail; for this you must look to Pevsner, or to various other published descriptions of varying quality. I shall do no more than indicate a few features of notable beauty and, I trust, of general interest to any town visitor.

The Minster belongs essentially to what has been aptly called the springtime of the Gothic style, like the cathedrals of Lincoln and Salisbury. Most of the building activity occurred during two periods: between *c.* 1235 and *c.* 1270, which saw the erection of the choir and both pairs of transepts, designs of exquisite purity and cool reticence (219), and between 1308 and 1349, when the unknown architect here did exactly what the great Henry Yeveley was to do over half a century later at Westminster Abbey, which was to continue the nave in what was in all essentials the same style: the Early English style, as it is now called. There is, surely, a lesson of wide application here for architects today. If completing or restoring, say, a Georgian terrace, the right course must be to do so in the same style. There is nothing to be ashamed of about this. On the contrary, it is a case of architectural good manners, of knowing where to be self-effacing as a mark of respect to the work of a predecessor. The earlier work must, of course, be worthy of that respect. But modern architects are often all too concerned to

220. Beverley Minster from the north-west

leave their own imprint, even on an old building not conditioned aesthetically to receive it. Victorian architects constantly did this too, but the dangers today are greater because of the new principles of design arising out of the employment of new materials: concrete, steel, and immense areas of glass. Hence, for example, the quite unnecessary destruction of the unity of some of the squares in London and elsewhere. It is a selfish, insensitive way of proceeding, a solecism not committed at Beverley.

There was a third period of vigorous building activity, between *c.* 1390 and *c.* 1420, but this only affected the church's extremeties. The new additions were the huge East window, so dramatic from without, the soaring North porch, profusely panelled, with a chamber above; and the superb West front (220), which is beyond doubt one of the most admirably composed church façades in the country. These are all mature examples of Perpendicular, the glorious last phase of English Gothic; but it was still Gothic, so no damage was done.

To step into the recently cleaned nave (221) is to experience a church interior of astonishing richness and with a lovely stylistic unity, and the beautiful Magnesian limestone can now again be seen in all its pristine perfection. But in those parts of the church dating from the thirteenth century another stone is very much in evidence: Purbeck marble, which is not really a marble at all but a very fossily limestone that will take a polish: that is the reason for the name. It is seen to especially telling effect in the slender columns of the exquisite double staircase in the North choir aisle (223), which was the way up into the octagonal Chapter House until that building was demolished in 1550. But Purbeck marble was used in profusion all over the choir and transepts, and that is the main respect in which the later nave differs from the rest.

The view from the crossing (225) is very revealing. Here we can take stock of the aesthetic significance of this dark Purbeck stone. Clearly its purpose was to emphasise the architectural structure of the building, which it certainly does. Some people like it; others find its dark tone over-emphatic. One bay west of the crossing, except at the level of the clerestory, it stops, and even though the design remains unchanged, the difference of effect is very striking. The renunciation of the Purbeck stone was not because of the cost of bringing it all the way from Dorset. It was due to a change of fashion at the beginning of the fourteenth century, which affected English church architecture everywhere.

The design of the triforium, which was certainly inspired by Lincoln, is a good example of the exuberance which was one aspect of thirteenth-century architecture. There are two contrasted arcades, set one in front of the other in a kind of counterpoint, the spandrels of the inner one being pierced with quatrefoils. The arches are elaborately moulded, with plenty of dog-tooth ornamentation; the effect is lavish.

The vault webs are all plastered over (222), and in the nave the charming painted decoration done at the time of the Victorian restoration has recently been freshened up. The ribs are of stone.

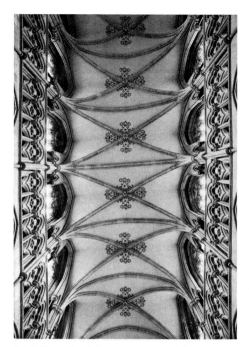

222. Beverley Minster, Nave Vault

221. Beverley Minster, Nave, looking east

223. Beverley Minster, stairs to vanished Chapter House

224. The great treadwheel

225. Beverley Minster. Nave, north side from the crossing

What cannot be known from below, and what indeed comes as a great surprise, is that the infilling of the vault is brick. To see this it is necessary to ascend one of the towers and penetrate the ample space between the vault and the high roof. For those concerned with materials, this is of great historical interest. For there is hardly any brickwork in the country as early as this – it is well over 600 years old – and certainly there is none so well preserved.

From this lofty vantage point it is quite easy to step out through a door on to the parapet, from which a vivid impression can be obtained of the profusion of carved stonework which adorns the upper parts of this marvellous building. This stone was not carved *in situ*. It was prepared in the mason's yard. So it all had to be hauled up by rope and pulley with the aid of a winch; at the bigger churches, like this one, the winch was part and parcel of a large wheel (224). Only three of these great treadwheels now survive: two in cathedrals – Canterbury and Salisbury – and this one at Beverley. (Peterborough has a smaller one.) This oak wheel, which is nearly 15 feet in diameter, has in fact little or no wood in it earlier than 1700, but it was still in use until 1977. It is situated above the vault of the central tower, and whenever a load needs to be lifted up, a wooden 'plug' can be removed. Today the work is done by an

226. Beverley Minster, looking West from the Percy screen

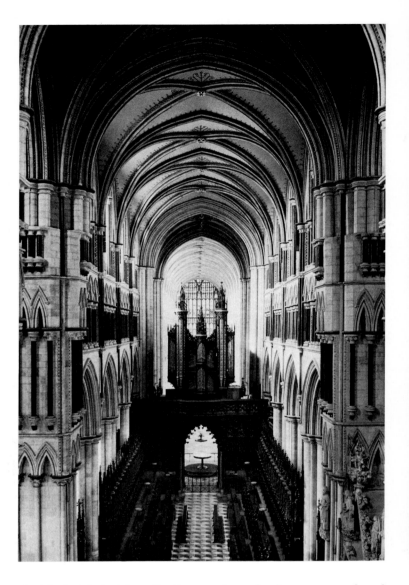

electric hoist; but happily the wooden wheel, a very good and faithful servant, has not been dismantled.

In the choir the reredos, behind the high altar, abuts on to what is known as the Percy screen, much restored in 1825, but still an exquisite survival from the Decorated period. It is entirely stone, with a flat top accessible by a tiny winding staircase from the north choir aisle. On this, until the Dissolution, was exhibited the Minster's most revered treasure, the gold and silver shrine of St John of Beverley, wrought by a London goldsmith in the 1290s and thereafter an object of pilgrimage and a valuable source of church income. Needless to say, no trace of the shrine survives, but the platform on which it stood provides a splendid vantage point from which to view the church.

Prominent in the westward prospect (226) are the sumptuous though much repaired Tudor stalls with no fewer than sixty-eight misericords. The screen was designed by Sir Gilbert Scott, and so was

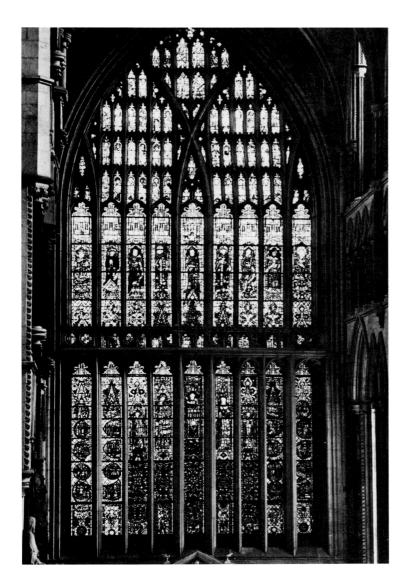

the organ case, which incorporates parts of an earlier one built by Johann Snetzler in the 1760s. Scott's craftsman was James Elwell, a well-known character in Victorian times at Beverley. It is very well done, if the organ must be placed here, which personally I deplore as it interferes with the perspective view of the vault. The marble floor is a fascinating example of *trompe l'oeil*, and dates from the thorough, and on the whole unusually good, eighteenth-century restoration.

In the other direction there is a grandstand view of the great Perpendicular East window, of nine lights (227). This harbours the only medieval glass in the Minster to have survived. Of many different dates, it was all collected and inserted here with some contemporary additions in 1725. It is a beautiful kaleidoscope of fragments, and from a little way off looks lustrous and rich; but it provides only faint, tantalising clues to the former glories of which, through human folly and bigotry, the church was later deprived. The loss of the old glass was a great tragedy.

228. Beverley Minster, Percy tomb, detail of canopy

On the north side of the high altar is the Percy tomb, which has been described as 'the most splendid of all British Decorated funerary monuments'. Oddly enough it is not known who is commemorated, for there is no effigy: the most likely candidate is Lady Idonea Percy, who died in 1365. The canopy (228) takes the form of a pair of cusped ogee arches set within steep gables. The elaboration of the carving is prodigious, and, surprisingly, it escaped the attentions of the iconoclasts. In France the stained glass would have had a better chance of survival but, as this was the tomb of an aristocrat, the sculpture would almost certainly have been smashed to bits in 1789. Its loss would have been deplorable; nevertheless, had I been given the choice of sacrificing one or the other, I would certainly have kept the glass. This is a judgment of general application throughout the English cathedrals and churches.

At the Reformation the Minster had seventy-seven people on the foundation: canons, parsons, chantry priests (fifteen of these), clerks, vicars-choral and choristers, sextons, acolytes and a variety of others. In 1547 these were reduced to four. But the confiscation of the church's endowments was a very serious matter for its future. How could the vast fabric be maintained? Fortunately, for once, a good solution was found. About 1552 responsibility for the Minster was handed over to the Corporation, and some of the lands were given back; in 1579 the Crown returned some more. For nearly three centuries – until 1835 – the Minster was maintained by the Corporation out of these revenue-producing estates. Largely for that reason it was better looked after in the eighteenth century than almost any other church in England, including most of the cathedrals.

In the field of woodwork the early years of the eighteenth century brought some notable additions. These included the west doors with, on their inner face, panels bearing excellent figures of the four Evangelists, carved in oak by the Thorntons of York, and a spectacular, somewhat Baroque font cover (229), with eight cherub's heads, scrolls, and, at the apex, a dove; it hangs from a delightful wrought iron suspension rod. From *c.* 1716 to 1720 the architect in charge was Nicholas Hawksmoor. Not everything he did was good: he introduced a Gothick screen in stone, an altar canopy in the Corinthian style, and galleries in the aisles of the nave. No regrets need be felt, I believe, that all these were long ago swept away; and it seems that Hawksmoor was also responsible for the strange onion-like cupola erected at this time over the low central tower. This was removed, and most people would say rightly, in 1824. It is seen in a watercolour by J. C. Buckler (230) preserved in the Art Gallery.

The maintenance of this vast church is an intimidating responsibility for a town with fewer than twenty thousand inhabitants and, as has been observed, relatively few visitors. But the challenge has been accepted, and in recent years yet another ambitious programme of restoration has been carried out, notably

229. Beverley Minster, font and cover

230. Beverley Minster, early 19th-century watercolour by J. C. Buckler

231. Water Pump, North Bar Within

on the stonework, which is now in a far better state than it has been for many generations. The work still continues.

St Mary (232), near the other end of the town, is a splendid parish church in its own right, and quite independent of the Minster. In any other town of this size, it would almost certainly be the dominant building. This was the church favoured by the merchant guilds, so it received many bequests. But on 29 April 1520, during the morning service, the old Norman tower suddenly collapsed, killing many of the worshippers, as a mutilated inscription in the church still records. So the present noble tower is a Tudor creation, as indeed is the major part of the church. The material is again Magnesian limestone from near Tadcaster. The interior is chiefly memorable for the chapel of St Michael, which occupies the north aisle of the chancel. This is a fine piece of late-Decorated building (c. 1330–40), with exquisite tracery in the windows and a rich tierceron vault: the only part of the church to have been vaulted. Happily it was not damaged when the tower fell.

Historic Beverley is a long narrow place (216), and much of what is best worth seeing lies in the area between these two churches. In the Middle Ages this was much the largest town in East Yorkshire. In 1377, which was just about the time when the prosperity of the town was at its highest, the population was probably about five thousand. This meant that, although only half the size of York, it was more than twice as large as Hull.

The explanation of the elongated plan is, as so often, rooted in geology. For it is here that the chalk Wolds drop into the Boulder clay of Holderness. The chalk is porous: the clay more or less impermeable. So along the line of junction there bubbled forth a succession of springs, and a good water supply invariably attracted the early settlers. Beverley has always possessed this. In the Middle Ages, and indeed for a long time after, there were streams running along many of the streets, which is why to this day they are so winding. The 'pleasant springs running through the streets' were a subject of comment in a letter written by Daniel Defoe in 1726. So at one time the town had many water pumps. In North Bar Within can still be seen, deprived now of its handle, a solitary survivor (231).

Until macadamising came in, the streets were paved with stone setts, as Highgate, which faces the Minster's North porch, still is. Highgate is but one of the street names here ending in 'gate'. Others include Hengate, Ladygate, Lairgate, Keldgate, Minster Moorgate, Eastgate, Flemingate and Walkergate, alongside which flowed the town's principal stream, the Walker Beck, in which the cloth was 'walked' through the water to wash it. We have already encountered a street with the same name, and for the same reason, at Berwick, where I pointed out that 'gate' is by derivation a Norse word quite unconnected with any notion of gating.

Beverley did, however, have its gates, which were known here as Bars. In the Middle Ages there were five of them, of which only

232. St Mary's Church

three were still standing when Leland came here about 1540: even the exact locations of South Bar and Norwood Bar are uncertain. Of the others, Newbegin Bar survived until 1790 and Keldgate Bar until 1808. North Bar still stands (233), and long may it continue to do so, for it is now performing a most valuable service to the town as an obstruction to heavy traffic. Oddly enough, unlike Hull and, of course, York, Beverley never had any walls; only a town ditch. So, except perhaps for collecting tolls, the Bars in the past were really more decorative than useful.

The North Bar was built in 1409. Although that is two generations later than the vault over the Minster's nave, it is still an exceptionally early example of English brickwork. The bricks were made locally by about twenty brickmakers, and the number required was 112,300. This is known as, remarkably enough, the accounts have survived. The size varies somewhat, but the average is about $9 \times 4\frac{1}{2} \times 2$ inches. Some are as much as ten inches long. They are not all very true, so the mortar courses have to be fairly wide; and inevitably there have been some replacements. Nor are many of the bricks red: the majority are brownish. Especially remarkable about this gate, at so early a date, are the refinements: on both faces there are three blind windows with heads which, though modest indeed compared with the canopy of the Percy tomb, are also of cusped ogee form; and, higher up, there is a saw-tooth string course, achieved by laying the bricks diagonally to expose one corner of each, held between two slightly projecting courses. It sounds simple enough, but it is very effective, and admirably suited to the material. The crow-step battlements above are framed between plain gabled pilasters rising from corbels. Nowhere else in England can any comparable resourcefulness in the handling of brick be found at so early a date.

The long narrow town was for centuries fringed with pastures. Those to the east stretched to the banks of the River Hull, by which, until its waters were controlled during the eighteenth century, they were constantly flooded. Today most of them are covered with houses and, beyond, industrial buildings, and are of no artistic interest.

To the west, on the other hand, the grassland survives intact and is a great asset to the town. Beverley was very fortunate in its overlords, the Archbishops of York. As early as 1129 Archbishop Thurstan had granted the citizens a charter, one of the oldest extant (and still preserved in the Corporation archives), which gave them exemption from tolls throughout Yorkshire and other privileges. In 1380 Archbishop Neville granted the Pasture of Westwood, an area of about 600 acres, to the burgesses of Beverley in perpetuity, at an annual rent of £5. This was a wonderful gift. Not only did they get free grazing; the Westwood yielded chalk – very valuable to the builders for lime, timber and firewood. In 1750 each freeman could graze four cows or two horses. Today the Westwood is an immense recreation ground, with a golf course, a

gallop for racehorses, and that wonderful view of the town with the towers of the two churches, referred to earlier. The Race Course, first laid out in the 1690s, is just to the north.

Originally the principal value of the Westwood was for the grazing of sheep. Not only was wool exported, but at a very early date the town was already weaving cloth. As early as 1236 (which was well ahead of Bradford-on-Avon), the cloths of Beverley were so well known that Henry III ordered a number for his personal use. The wolds were now given over almost entirely to sheep farming, which brought great prosperity in its wake. The town still bears many evidences of the impact of the wool trade. In Westwood Road there is to this day an inn called the Wool Pack. Among the street names there are Walkergate, referred to above, Flemingate, at the south-east end of the town which was exactly the route that Flemish traders would have followed, and Dyer Lane, which speaks for itself. Another flourishing industry, the most important after cloth-making, was tanning. For this a plentiful supply of tree bark was needed in addition to abundant water, and Beverley could provide both.

The perpetual source of anxiety was Hull, which had the

234. Market Cross

advantage of a big river, and from 1299 the patronage of the King. In that year Edward I granted it the right to handle for export the entire output of Yorkshire's woollen and leather goods, and to call itself Kingston (King's Town)-upon-Hull. Beverley's vital artery, the River Hull, flowed through Hull to reach the sea. Thus her rival could, if so disposed, throttle her; and ultimately this is very much what happened. As early as the 1540s the ancient ferry over the river at Hull was replaced by a bridge. The central section of this bridge could be slid back to enable masted vessels to pass through. But if the Hullensians did not choose to open their bridge, or imposed exorbitant tolls for doing so, the Beverlonians (I am a stickler, you will observe, for the correct terms) were stymied.

This state of affairs persisted until 1846 when, at last, Beverley got its railway line. By then it was too late. It may well be that the railway proved more useful to Hull than to Beverley. The small, beautiful town has become increasingly a select dormitory for the industrial and mercantile emporium, as well as for some of the academics.

But this is to anticipate. After the decline in Beverley's fortunes during the fifteenth century and a long period of decay throughout the time of the Tudors, the town gradually began to recover some of its former prosperity, owing to the influx of new industries. The wool and cloth trades were now dead: clothing in Yorkshire had long since shifted to the West Riding, to Leeds and Bradford, Halifax and Wakefield. Tanning, it is true, continued; the last tannery only closed its doors very recently. But the town was surrounded by rich farming land, and already in 1697 Celia Fiennes was remarking that it had 'three markets, one for Beasts, another for Corne, and another for Fish, all large'. Especially in the eighteenth century, agriculture was very flourishing. Brickmaking, in decline since the Middle Ages, now made a spirited revival. There was also lace. 'The poor people,' observed Defoe, 'mostly support themselves now by working bone-lace, which of late has met with particular encouragement.' Even the children 'were maintained at school to work this sort of lace'.

The town also changed its character, becoming in the eighteenth century, like, among other places, Lewes and Ludlow, a desirable centre for the local gentry. Here geography was a help. Apart from Hull, there was nowhere else for them to go if they wanted, as they did, Assembly Rooms, a theatre and a race course. York was five or six hours' ride away. Thus many of them maintained, as secondary residences, principally for use in the winter when the roads were very bad, town houses of considerable elegance, as we shall see. Many of the best houses were built for doctors and lawyers, as well as for merchants, bankers and local landowners. The town had two Members of Parliament. (This endured until 1870.) It also preserved its ancient immunity from tolls and customs duties: the people of Beverley, noted Defoe, 'pay nothing in any port or town in England'. A most valuable privilege. So it is no surprise to discover that, apart from its churches, historic Beverley is predominantly a Georgian creation.

Away from the churches, stone is a rarity here. The only local variety is chalk. At the delightful Market Cross (234), erected in 1714, the columns are stone, but they decayed so badly that they had to be rendered with cement.

Otherwise this structure is mostly wood, with a protective covering of lead on the roof. Wood has been a very important material in Beverley, but a great deal of it is internal, or hidden behind Georgian face-lifts in brick or plaster. Even before the end of the fourteenth century Hull, according to Leland, had 'most part of the houses of the Towne made of brike'; but this was not true of Beverley, nor indeed of any other English town at that time or for long after. Timber-framing was the rule for every house here at least until the end of the sixteenth century. So it is perhaps surprising that only about three examples of pre-1600 timbered buildings have managed to survive, all considerably altered. The best one (235), although at ground level now a garage, has stone and brick infilling, which has been whitewashed, between the studs.

235. 49–51 North Bar Within

236. 4–6 North Bar Without

At the end of the nineteenth century there was, it is true, an outbreak of black-and-white, principally outside the North Bar. The houses illustrated (236) date from 1892–4, and were designed by the same James Elwell who had worked for Scott on the organ screen of the Minster. The unexpected painted decoration on the cove is rather enjoyable. Otherwise they leave us feeling very thankful that this phase at Beverley was short-lived, for these buildings seem painfully out of place here. They look as if, in a fit of absent-mindedness, they had bounced across from Chester.

Apart from this aberration, Beverley today is pre-eminently a

237. Newbegin House, 16 Newbegin

brick town. There were abundant deposits of material suitable for making bricks and tiles readily available on the Boulder clay just to the East. Not that all the bricks produced, which tend to be of a somewhat brownish red, were of specially good quality: some, in fact, were decidedly poor, and today crumble to the touch. But from the upturn in the town's fortunes after the Restoration this was the accepted material for the better houses. And by the end of the seventeenth century its employment had become general. Of the earlier examples, Newbegin House (237), situated in a specially delightful street for the study of brick, is among the most stately.

Beverley's brick houses of the Queen Anne and Georgian periods add up to something that is really very rewarding. In this book it is only possible to illustrate and comment on a few of them. Two of the most characteristic, both dating from between 1730 and 1740 (precise dating of these houses is often difficult), are 38 Highgate (238) and 62 North Bar Without, also known as Ash Close (239). These two gracious houses, separated by the whole length of the town, are basically similar yet exhibit many delightful differences of detail. 38 Highgate served from 1740 to 1890 as the Blue Coat School. Except in the dormers, all the windows preserve their original glazing bars. Immediately below the upper range runs a plat-band capped with stone which incorporates the sills. The window-heads are of finer, gauged brick, and in the shadow under the eaves there is a cornice with brick modillions. Ash Close, which was the town house of the Sykes family of Sledmere, is somewhat grander, especially inside. The central bay breaks forward a little. The windows, which, apart from the fanlight, were reglazed at the end of the eighteenth century (observe the thinner bars), are loftier and have projecting keystones. The window-heads are again of gauged brick but have here been whitened, as has the arch over the door which frames a very simple fanlight. There is no plat-band here and the cornice is an early nineteenth-century replacement. At both houses the dormer windows have no sash-cords but slide

238. 38 Highgate

239. Ash Close, 62 North Bar Without

38

39

sideways, as do all the windows in many humbler houses of the Georgian period.

The roofs make an interesting contrast, wholly typical of Beverley at this time. The old timber-framed houses had all been thatched. With the advent of brick-making, tiles were made too, and, before long, pantiles. These have already been described in the chapter on Berwick (p. 60), where it was noted that they are specially characteristic of the east and north-east of England, although quite common also in Somerset (p. 148). At Beverley they provide one of the town's greatest visual assets, far superior to the bricks, and the roof of 38 Highgate, which directly faces the Minster, is a typically engaging example. The warm colour and rich texture of these pantiles is a constant pleasure here, even more so than at Berwick, because there are many more of them. Moreover they are still being employed. Some if not all of the pantiles used in Beverley today are made, by hand, at Goxhill, which is on the right bank of the Humber, opposite Hull.

With such a delightful roofing material at hand locally, it might be supposed that there could be no good reason for making a change. Such a view takes no account of that fickle jade, fashion. During the nineteenth century Westmorland slates became available. They were more expensive than pantiles, but their attractive colours, often blue-grey, exercised a great appeal. So those who could afford them sometimes installed them, and that is why Ash Close has a roof of graded slates. It is a good roof, but does not 'belong' here as the pantiles do.

Both earlier and later than the foregoing is 7 Hengate (240). This was originally a Queen Anne house, built in 1709. The quoins and the coping of the projecting base are of stone, painted; the brickwork (the base English bond, the rest Flemish: cf. pages 84 and 86) has suffered in various ways, especially from inept repointing. In 1785 the original doorcase was replaced by the present one in the Tuscan Doric style, elegant if slightly attenuated; the charming little wrought-iron hand-rails, with foot-scrapers attached, also date from this time. The windows are old but not original, nor all of the same date, and are worth studying.

Sash-framed windows only become general in the South during the reign of Queen Anne, and to reach the North took longer. Although few now survive, Ivan and Elisabeth Hall affirm that leaded casements, sometimes with a mullion and a transom, were standard practice at Beverley until the 1740s.[*]

Long before this – to be precise, in 1709 – an Act of Parliament had enacted that sash-framed windows in London, instead of being flush with the wall surface, must be set back four inches within a reveal to counter the danger of fire. The Statute was not made obligatory elsewhere but other towns, perceiving its practical value, gradually followed suit. At 7 Hengate the downstairs windows, which would also appear to date from 1785, are still set in delicately moulded frames in the same plane as the wall. Upstairs there is a difference. The pair on the right are somewhat earlier, and the frames are plainer, but these, too, are flush with the wall. Not so, however, the left-hand pair, which are set back within a shallow reveal, although the actual windows appear identical with the other pair. It need scarcely be added that the machine-made tiles are recent.

Another Act of Parliament, passed in 1707 and also concerned with fire danger, proscribed wooden cornices, but this again applied only to London. There were, as we shall see, plenty of wooden cornices in Beverley throughout the eighteenth century; that at the Beverley Arms (242), just below the parapet, dates only from 1794. In that year the building was reconstructed by the leading builder in the town during the latter part of the century, William Middleton, who started life as a joiner and lived to become four times Mayor. The chief feature is the spacious doorway, with Tuscan Doric columns, fluted capitals, a very graceful fanlight, and an arched window above framed by a stone architrave, and all part

---

[*] *Historic Beverley* (William Sessions, York, 1973), p. 51. This very well illustrated book is indispensable for the serious student of the architecture of Beverley. I have been much indebted not only to their book but to Dr and Mrs Hall personally in the writing of this chapter.

241. 55–63 North Bar Within

of the same composition. The windows here are set back within reveals; but a little farther along the same street, North Bar Within, a terrace of five houses (241) dating from *c.* 1780, and perhaps also by Middleton, has its windows still nearly flush with the walls. The two canted bays are unfortunate later alterations, but it should also be said, with warm approval, that in two of these houses the glazing bars, replaced in the Victorian period by sheet glass, have lately been put back. The visual benefit is quite startling, the more so as this is a terrace. Very agreeable are the five identical and slightly 'Adamish' doorcases, and the wrought-iron hand-rails recalling the pair at 7 Hengate.

The relative affluence of the town during the eighteenth century was reflected, as so often, in the foundation of several almshouses, not all of which any longer serve their original purpose. One such is Tymperon House in Walkergate (243). Built about 1732, this former almshouse has recently had to be (very successfully) re-roofed, but the windows still preserve their original Crown glass. The special feature, however, is the trio of lofty recessed arches, with stone bases and imposts. The upper-storey windows have segmental heads in order to fit neatly underneath. These arches give strength and dignity to what is by no means a large house.

It is not known who designed this house, but it is evident that the front elevation fascinated James Moyser, who in 1748 was responsible for Ann Routh's Hospital in Keldgate (244). Moyser

242. Beverley Arms Hotel. 25–27 North Bar Within

was the son of Beverley's Member of Parliament in Queen Anne's time, a man of substance and an Army colonel, whose interest in architecture was no doubt fostered by his friendship with Lord Burlington. Not much of the work of this amateur is known, but it is evident that he was indebted to others for his ideas. Here he was acting for the Corporation, who had received a bequest from Mrs Ann Routh Moore to build and endow a hospital 'for the maintenance of twelve poor old women of the parishes of St John [the Minster] and St Martin, frequenting the Church'. The principal difference from Tymperon House is in the introduction of a pediment over the full width of the elevation, edged with moulded stone and containing a delightful Rococo cartouche: a painted coat of arms framed by cornucopia, palm leaves and scrolls. And although the photograph does not show it, this is another building with a roof of graded Westmorland slates.

The recessed arch motif was to become something of a Beverley speciality during the succeeding hundred years or so. It can even be seen at the goods warehouse adjoining the Railway Station.

The larger Georgian houses were set in very spacious grounds. Some of these survive, but those of Lairgate Hall (245) were mostly built over between the wars, after the house itself had become the Municipal Offices. This was long the home of the Pennymans, of whom Sir James, the 5th baronet, was one of Beverley's MPs from 1774 to 1790. It was built about 1700 but much altered in the

24

24

1760s and again later. Everything here is of the best quality. Stone is much more in evidence than is usual at Beverley. There are the strong moulded base, the centre-piece (added not earlier than 1780), the large keystones over the windows, the quoins, and the roof of, again, graded Westmorland slates, with lead for the ridges. The modillioned eaves cornice is of wood. The dormers here are better than any that we have seen elsewhere. The interior was also of considerable elegance; but, alas, office use and elegance are not usually compatible. The Council, all the same, is very lucky to be able to work in so distinguished a building.

243. Tymperon House, 62 Walkergate

244. Ann Routh's Hospital, 28 Keldgate

245. Lairgate Hall

No less fortunate are the girls of the former High School, which is now comprehensive, although not co-educational. They occupy the building known as Norwood House (246), once the home of a family named, I presume fortuitously, Beverley. The builder, about 1765, Jonathan Midgley, was a prosperous attorney who twice became the town's mayor, and it seems probable that his architect was Thomas Atkinson, who is now known to have designed Sutton Hall, north of York, which is somewhat similar. On the entrance front the whole of the ground floor is faced with stone, laid in rusticated blocks. In addition, each alternate block on either side of the door is vermiculated: that is to say, given a surface intended to suggest the tracks of worms. Miraculously, the contemporary wrought-iron torch-holders are also still *in situ*. But of course the dominant feature of this elevation is the huge pediment, spreading

246. Norwood House

here not over three bays but five, with a profusion of wooden modillions. The big Rococo cartouche frames an *oeil de boeuf* window, and festoons of linked husks hang out from either side. The garden front (248) is comparable but much plainer; if two of the windows had later to be carried down to the ground it is a pity that the other pair were not treated similarly. There have been many additions; the projecting wing on the left with the enormous windows was, and indeed still is, a library, added about 1825 by Alderman William Beverley (whose father Robert was a first cousin of George Washington).

Within, the Drawing Room has survived more or less intact (247). Over the fireplace there is stucco panel comprising a sunburst with the heads of three winged cherubs in a very pretty Rococo frame. The other stucco decorations furnish a good example of the way in which ideas circulated during the eighteenth century. The inspirer of the ceiling design, as Dr Ivan Hall has pointed out, was the Palladian architect Colen Campbell; but he had been dead for forty years. This design was for a ceiling at Compton Place, Eastbourne, which was included in a well-known pattern book, *The Modern Builder's Assistant*, that appeared in 1757; and it seems virtually certain that this was the book to which the Beverley stuccoist turned.

Of almost exactly the same date, but utterly different in character, is the stucco decoration in the Court Room of the Guildhall (250). This must surely be the most elegant room not only in Beverley but for many miles around. Perhaps rather surprisingly, in view of the austerity usually associated with the Law, the adornment is in the richest Rococo, far surpassing that of the Court Room at Warwick (38). The *stuccatore*, responsible not only for the lovely ceiling with the ground mainly dark blue, but

247. Norwood House, Drawing Room

248. Norwood House, garden front

249. Wrought-iron Staircase, St Mary's Manor, North Bar Within

250. Guildhall, Court Room

also for the sumptuous Royal Arms, was an Italian, Giuseppe Cortese.

Under the Royal Arms is the seat of the Mayor, who was also the Chief Magistrate. This is set within a boldly decorative wooden frame carved by Edmund Foster of Hull. It was seemingly inspired by a design in a famous pattern book, Thomas Chippendale's *Director*. At the other end of the room is a gallery, below which is a pair of Doric columns which from *c.* 1720 to 1826 could be seen in the Minster.

Another 'throw-out' from the Minster can be seen at St Mary's Manor, a large early nineteenth-century stucco-faced house now leased by the County Council to the Ministry of Agriculture and Fisheries. The staircase landing (249) has four fine wrought-iron panels which, Mr G. Philip Brown, the Borough Librarian, has all but proved, were originally part of the altar rails provided for the Minster in the early 1720s. That was just after the time when Hawksmoor had been the Minster architect, and it is therefore significant that the altar rails in his church of St Mary Woolnoth in the City of London are of strikingly similar design. These rails, it is now known, were the work of a London smith named John Robins. Whether he also made the panels at Beverley, or whether some other smith copied the design, is the one uncertainty. Where there is no room for doubt is that in 1825 they were thrown out of the Minster for not being Gothic. They were bought, for £39 4s., by Mr Henry Ellison, who then owned St Mary's Manor. Not only did he have them installed on the landing; he also had more panels made *en suite* for the balustrade of the staircase. The effect is extremely handsome.

The staircases are one of the special features of Beverley's many Georgian interiors. A spacious and well-carved staircase, like the one illustrated here (251), can make a good contribution to the character of a house. Nowadays, no doubt, some people would regard such things as a great waste of space. I certainly would not: a fine staircase would give me aesthetic pleasure every time I went up and down. The variations in the design of the balusters are a

251. Staircase, Ash Close, 62 North Bar Without

252. Staircase, 11 Saturday Market

constant source of enjoyment. The corkscrew, on an elaborate base, was one of the favourite motifs, and occurs in quite a modest house (252) built about 1755 for a local clockmaker. One should look at the handrails and at the tread-ends too. Over and over again the craftsmanship is a delight. But because they are all private, few people will have access to these staircases, or even be aware of their existence.

Beverley is, however, also a very good town in which to look at cornices, and here, since they are external, there is no problem of access. The purpose of the cornice was partly aesthetic but, outside, functional too. Until the advent of gutters and downpipes, not usually introduced before the eighteenth century, a projecting eaves, with a cornice below, served to ensure that rainwater falling on the roof was thrown well clear of the wall. Never mind who might be walking underneath; when it was raining it was up to them to keep clear. Unfortunately the effectiveness of many good cornices, like the bold one at Newbegin House (237), dating from about 1690, was later marred by the addition of lead or iron gutters.

Cornices could be of wood, plaster or brick; all three materials can frequently be seen at Beverley, and contemporaneously. The great vogue for them lasted from roughly 1680 to 1800. During the Georgian period the modillions, or brackets, tended to get smaller. Wood is the commonest material for these cornices: typical examples on a large scale have already been encountered at Lairgate Hall (245) and at Norwood House (246, 248). Among more modest instances there are many variations. At 119

Walkergate (254) the modillions are given an ogee form, with a break across the centre. At 17 Highgate (255) they are somewhat similar, but with the additional embellishment of *guttae*, triplets of cone-shaped drops, hung like little tassels at the base of each. 8 Newbegin (256) has, in addition to modillions, a course of dentils, small rectangular blocks suggesting a row of teeth. 3 Newbegin (253) has dentils only, which produce a very delicate effect. In brick, dentillation tends to be clumsier: 51–53 Toll Gavel (257) is a mid-eighteenth-century example. A few yards farther on, at No. 69 (258), there is a pleasing variation: the saw-tooth moulding, which had been introduced centuries before, as we have seen, at the North Bar. Since it is so easy to achieve in brick, it seems to me a great pity that saw-toothing is so seldom employed today, because a moulding, however simple, always provides a good 'punctuation point' at the top of a wall. In both these examples the bricks have been painted, cream and white respectively. When the cornice casts a shadow, this certainly enhances their visibility.

254–258. Top to bottom: 119 Walkergate; 17 Highgate; 8 Newbegin; 51–53 Toll Gavel; 69 Toll Gavel

253. 3 Newbegin

259. Sessions House

260. County Record Office, Cross Street

259

260

Two more materials remain to be mentioned: white bricks and rendered stucco, both specially associated with the first half of the nineteenth century.

White bricks, so called, we have already encountered at Saffron Walden and at Lewes. They became fashionable, here as in so many other English towns, shortly before 1800, because their quiet colour could recall stone, as red bricks never could. These bricks, which are in fact pale yellow, are made, as was observed earlier (p. 88), with clay dug from the Gault; the chief source of supply for Beverley was near the banks of the Humber at Broomfleet, some fifteen miles upstream from Hull. Among many nineteenth-century buildings in this material, none is more imposing than the Sessions House (259) in New Walk, set back from the highway behind fine trees, which include one of the largest and most magnificent sycamores in England. The designer was Charles Watson of York, who at this time (1804–14) was the leading architect in Yorkshire. Here, it is true, the Gault brick of the building itself plays very much second fiddle to the imposing neo-Greek frontispiece, a tetrastyle portico in the Ionic style, which is built of biscuit-coloured Coal Measures sandstone brought all the way from the neighbourhood of Leeds. The Royal Arms adorns the pediment, which is crowned by a triumphant figure of Justice in Coade's artificial stone with gilded scales.

Some architectural writers are inclined to be patronising about stucco. I can never understand why. Admittedly it demands a high standard of maintenance; neglected, it quickly looks shoddy. It is

261. 11 Cross Street

also more at home in towns than in the country, and much better in a Classical than in a Gothic context. But it has made its own quite distinctive contribution to the architecture of Beverley. The County Record Office (260) in Cross Street was built about 1831 as a club. Did ever a building only one storey high and with only one window to either side of the entrance wear an air of greater authority? The portico has a pair of columns set *in antis*: that is to say, in the same plane as the flanking walls. Thus there is a pool of shadow at the centre and the brightest light plays over the rest. The elegantly glazed windows are framed by eared architraves which are carried down to the projecting base of the building to embrace, below each window, a moulded panel. It is a design of the most fastidious distinction.

And nearly opposite, also stuccoed throughout, is a private house, 11 Cross Street (261). Here the whole centre is slightly recessed, and there is the low pitched roof, hipped and slated, with the extremely wide eaves which are often the hallmark of this style. The architraves of the lower windows are again carried down to embrace panels, here lightly inset. The symmetry is precise to the smallest detail, which is exactly as it should be. And the stucco itself provides an impeccable finish for what is, surely, a little gem of late-Regency architecture.

Because the Minster is so glorious, many visitors to Beverley allow themselves little time to see anything else. It is my hope that this far from complete account will serve to reveal that there is a great deal here of high architectural quality. In some of the streets the traffic is bad, but others are reasonably quiet and happily a by-pass is now under construction. So Beverley should not be rushed; like all towns of high quality, it should be explored at leisure and of course on foot. Several days might not be too many. For those who do not yet know this town but who can respond to the pleasures of architecture – and, thanks largely to the BBC, they would seem to me to be an ever-increasing number – there is here a great surprise in store. Even in the company of the excellent towns which are the subject of the present book, Beverley more than holds its own.

Index

The most important references are indicated in bold type; illustrations are in italic type, and the italic numbers, like the others, refer to pages. The plate numbers do not appear here.